KB268432

폴 셰링 원작 | Written by Matt Olmstead

PRISON BREAK

프리즌 브레이크 EPISODE-4

2007년 11월 13일 초판 1쇄

번역·해설 ǀ 이일범
펴 낸 이 ǀ 조치영
책임편집 ǀ 이수정
편   집 ǀ 윤정미
마 케 팅 ǀ 이준승, 이동헌
경영지원 ǀ 마하선
디 자 인 ǀ 리드컴퍼니 이윤영
인   쇄 ǀ 삼성인쇄주식회사
펴 낸 곳 ǀ 스크린영어사

서울특별시 관악구 신림 9동 1514번지
TEL ǀ (02)887-8416
FAX ǀ (02)887-8591
http://www.screenplay.co.kr

등록일자 ǀ 1997년 7월 9일
등록번호 ǀ 제16-1495

책값 12,000원
ISBN 978-89-87915-83-8

- 낙장, 파본은 교환해 드립니다.

Prison Break: Season One
"Cute Poison" Written by Matt Olmstead
Based on the series created by Paul T. Scheuring
Copyright © Twentieth Century Fox Film Corporation
All rights reserved.

The pictures from the drama are used
by permission of Twentieth Century Fox Film Corporation.

Korean edition is published
by arrangement with Twentieth Century Fox Film Corporation
through Duran Kim Agency.

PRISONBREAK

EPISODE-4

PREFACE

벌써 〈프리즌 브레이크〉 네 번째의 에피소드가 출간된다. 필자로서는 그 동안 출간된 〈프리즌 브레이크〉의 스크린 영어로 독자들이 얼마나 큰 소득을 얻었는지 궁금하다. 단지 드라마의 스릴과 치밀한 구성만을 즐겼는지, 아니면 그와 더불어 다양한 인물들의 주옥 같은 영어 대사를 듣고 터득하며 말해 보고 있는지, 각기 독자들을 만나 확인하고 싶은 마음 뿐이다. 혹시 어떤 영어 학습 교재보다 탁월하고 귀중한 영어 자료의 진가를 인식하지 못하거나 아니면 방법을 모르거나 의지 부족으로 투자한 금액의 수십 배 이익을 얻지 못하고 지나치고 있는 건 아닌지 한 분 한 분 독자들을 붙들고 확인하고 싶은 심정이다.

실제 모국어가 아닌 외국어를 새로이 습득하여 익숙하게 사용하는 경지에 다다른다는 것은 결코 쉬운 일이 아니다. 아울러 1, 2년에 성취할 수 있을 정도로 만만한 과정도 아니다. 그렇기 때문에 우리 주위에 영어를 아주 잘하는 사람들이 많은 것처럼 보이지만 실제로 파헤치고 보면 영어 능통자가 극히 소수에 불과하다는 사실을 알고 적잖이 놀랄 것이다. 즉, 영어 능통자가 되기 위해서 끊임없이 노력하는 사람들은 많아도 정말로 사회가 원하는 영어 능통자는 그다지 많지 않다는 말이 된다. 필자의 경우만 해도 영어에 쏟은 세월이 50년은 넘었지만 매일 영영 사전을 옆에 끼고 살고 있으며, 모르는 표현에 대해 원어민에게 묻거나 인터

넷을 뒤지고 있고, 특히 젊은 원어민들과 대화를 나눌 때면 대화가 막혀 식은땀이 흐르는 경우가 허다하다.

10년 전쯤 캐나다의 한 유명한 스키 리조트에서 그곳의 치과의사와 한 리프트를 타고 올라간 적이 있다. 서로 인사를 나누는 것이 관례인지라 가볍게 인사를 나눴는데 무심코 내 소개를 한 것이 화근이 될 줄은 몰랐다. 내가 한국에서 왔으며 대학의 영문과 교수라고 말하자 그는 마치 내가 자신의 캐나다인 친구인 것처럼 질문을 퍼대기 시작하는 것이 아닌가? 대화의 내용은 날씨나 생활 습관 등 일상적인 것이 아니라 양국의 정치, 경제와 사회 전반에 걸친 것이었다. 내가 좀 우물쭈물하면 그 사람은 그렇게 쉬운 말도 못 알아듣는 사람이 어떻게 대학에서 영어를 가르치느냐고 웃으면서 핀잔까지 주는 것이다. 물론 조크였지만 그날 따라 왜 그렇게 리프트를 타고 올라가는 시간이 그리 길던지….

아직도 필자는 영어 전반에 걸쳐 실력이 부족하지만 여러 독자들한테 마치 영어에 능숙한 양 책을 집필하고 있다. 하지만 필자는 자신의 영어 실력이 부족하다는 것을 알고 거의 매일 이 나이에도 영어와 씨름하고 있다. 독자 여러분! 영어 정복으로 가는 길은 이처럼 길고도 험난하다. 하지만 시간 나는 대로 스크린 영어 교재와 DVD를 끼고 입체적인 싸움을 계속한다면 여러분의 여정은 훨씬 더 평탄하고 즐거울 것이며 비교적 빠른 시일 내에 찬란한 빛을 맞이할 것이라고 확신한다.

CONTENTS

영어의 특징

　　영어의 쓰임에서나 수준에서나 에피소드 3과 크게 차이가 나지 않는다. 수크레가 마리크루즈와 벌이는 사랑 싸움에 사촌인 헥터까지 합세하여 역시 스페인어는 물론 그들의 말투가 등장하고, 수크레 대신 마이클의 감방 동료가 된 헤이와이어의 말에 등장하는 의학 용어가 어려운 편이다. 또 이 에피소드의 제목인 '짜릿한 독극물'이 보여주는 것처럼 마이클이 사용하는 화학 공식이나 화학 약품, 그리고 화학 반응을 통한 거품과 부식에 관한 어휘가 새롭고, 심심치 않게 등장하는 병의 이름이나 증세 등도 만만치 않으며, 베로니카가 링컨을 위해 전개하는 법정 용어 등이 생소하다.

　　정신 병동 출신의 수감자인 헤이와이어, 아버지의 누명을 교훈 삼아 베로니카의 일에 뛰어드는 닉까지 새로 합세한 인물들의 말 속도나 표현 등이 전체적으로 영어의 난이도를 올리는 계기가 된다. 작품 전체적으로 볼 때 전개 부분에 해당하는 에피소드이므로 역시 템포가 빠른 편이나 다행히 긴 대사는 없으므로 긴장감을 즐기면서 학습하는 데는 크게 문제가 없을 것이다.

영어 난이도 The Degree of Difficulty	★★★		
속도 Speed ★★★	표현 Expression ★★★★	어휘 Vocabulary ★★★★	

1

I'D BETTER GET TO PROJECT JUSTICE

PRISON BREAK

1. INT. LINCOLN'S CELL. NIGHT
Camera pans around the dark cell to settle on Lincoln. He lays on a bunk asleep. Suddenly the cell door clangs open and light floods the cell, awakening Lincoln. He sits up in shock and Bellick walks in.

BELLICK : On your feet.

Lincoln shields his eyes from the sudden bright light.

LINCOLN : What time is it?

BELLICK : Get up.

Another C.O. walks into the cell.

LINCOLN : What's goin' on?

C.O. : Let's go, Lincoln. On your feet.

The C.O. pulls him to his feet and out of his cell.

LINCOLN : Bellick!

C.O. : Move it.

LINCOLN : Bellick! Bellick! No, Bellick! Bellick!

He struggles but he's pulled out of the cell. Bellick locks the door behind him.

2. INT. DEATH ROW HALLWAY. NIGHT
Lincoln is walked down a corridor on death row between two C.O.s.
He struggles the entire way.

LINCOLN : Bellick, where you taking ...? Bellick, no!

1. 내부. 링컨의 감방. 밤

카메라가 어두운 감방을 돌아 링컨을 비춘다. 그는 침대 위에서 잠을 자고 있다. 갑자기 감방 문이 쾅 열리면서 빛이 감방으로 몰려 들어와 링컨을 깨운다. 그는 놀라서 일어나 앉고 벨릭이 들어온다.

벨 릭　　　： 일어나라.

링컨은 갑작스런 밝은 빛을 피하려고 눈을 가린다.

링 컨　　　： 몇 시야?
벨 릭　　　： 일어나.

또 한 사람의 교도관이 감방으로 걸어 들어온다.

링 컨　　　： 무슨 일입니까?
교도관　　　： 가자, 링컨. 일어나.

그 교도관은 그를 일으켜 세우며 감방 밖으로 끌고 나간다.

링 컨　　　： 벨릭!
교도관　　　： 움직여.
링 컨　　　： 벨릭! 벨릭! 안 돼요, 벨릭! 벨릭!

그는 발버둥을 치지만 감방 밖으로 끌려 나간다. 벨릭은 그가 나간 뒤 문을 잠근다.

2. 내부. 사형수 감방 복도. 밤

링컨이 두 교도관에게 이끌려 사형수 감방 복도로 걸어내려 온다. 그는 끌려오는 내내 저항을 한다.

링 컨　　　： 벨릭, 어디로 데려가는 겁니까…? 벨릭, 안 돼요!

■ **clang**

(무기 · 종 등이) 뎅그렁〔철거덩〕 하고 울리다
- to make a loud ringing sound like that of metal being hit
- to cause something to make this sound

■ **shield**

~을 보호하다, 감싸다, 방패로 막다

On your feet.

일어나.

▶ on one's feet은 '서서, 일어 서서, 기운을 회복하여'이 관용구로, 명령문으로 쓰여 '일어서.'의 의미이다.

3. INT. DEATH CHAMBER. **CONTINUOUS**
Another door is pulled open and Lincoln is dragged inside.
He begins to panic even more.

LINCOLN : No. Bellick, no. Bellick, no.

In front of him is the electric chair.

LINCOLN : I'm not ... please!

He's forced down into the chair.

LINCOLN : No, Bellick! No! Please.

The C.O.s strap him into the chair.

C.O. : Pull it up!

LINCOLN : No! No! I got a month left! Please!

A wet sponge is forced down on his head and water floods his face.

LINCOLN : Bellick!

He gives up his protestations and starts to mutter.

LINCOLN : Please ... Bellick.

3. 내부. 사형실. 계속
또 하나의 문이 당겨 열리면서 링컨이 안쪽으로 끌려 들어온다.
그는 더욱 더 공포에 떨기 시작한다.

링 컨   : 안 돼. 벨릭, 안 돼요. 벨릭, 안 돼.

그의 앞에 전기 의자가 놓여 있다.

링 컨   : 난… 제발!

그는 강제로 의자에 앉혀진다.

링 컨   : 안 돼요, 벨릭! 안 돼요! 제발.

교도관들이 그를 의자에 가죽끈으로 잡아 맨다.

교도관   : 그만해!
링 컨   : 안 돼요! 안 돼! 한 달 남았다고요! 제발!

젖은 스펀지가 그의 머리 위에 놓이고 물이 그의 얼굴 위로 넘친다.

링 컨   : 벨릭!

그는 항의를 포기하고 중얼거리기 시작한다.

링 컨   : 제발… 벨릭.

- **death chamber**
  사형실, 임종의 방

- **panic**
  허둥대다, 공포에 질리다

- **pull up**
  멈추다, 세우다, (옷깃)을 세우다
  - to stop

- **protestation**
  항의, 이의, 불복
  - a strong statement that something is true, especially when other people do not believe you

I got a month left!
한 달 남았다고요!

▶ A month is left to me., I have a month left., There is a month left.와 같은 표현임.

The helmet is tightened beneath his chin. Lincoln begins to hyperventilate. An electrical cord is fastened to the helmet. Task completed, the C.O.s walk away, leaving Lincoln, panting, in the chair. The one way mirror shows people watching this on the other side. Bellick walks over to Lincoln.

BELLICK : Make your peace, Lincoln.

He pulls a black hood down over Lincoln's face.

BELLICK : Let's get on with it.

In an external room, a C.O. drops the switch on the wall controlling the chair's electrical currents. Lincoln shudders.

4. INT. LINCOLN'S CELL. MORNING
Lincoln wakes up on his stomach from his nightmare. He sits up, unnerved and breathes heavily. Slowly he puts his head in his hands.

5. EXT. FOX RIVER PENITENTIARY. NIGHT

6. INT. MICHAEL'S CELL. MORNING
Michael sits beside the sink. He slides the bolt through the cracks in the concrete. There's a clang from outside and he looks up in alarm before continuing his work. A guard calls out.

C.O. #1 : (V.O.) Open on forty!

The cell door slides open and Michael jumps up, forcing the sink back in its original position. Haywire appears outside the cell and walks in. The C.O. stands to one side as Haywire pulls himself up on the bunk.

그의 턱 아래에 헬멧이 고정된다. 링컨은 크게 숨을 들이쉬기 시작한다. 전기 선이 헬멧에 고정된다. 일이 다 끝나자 교도관들은 의자에 앉아 헐떡거리는 링컨을 남겨두고 가버린다. 한쪽 방향만 비치는 거울이 반대편에서 이를 지켜보고 있는 사람들의 모습을 비춘다. 벨릭이 링컨에게 다가 선다.

벨 릭　　　 : 편히 잠들어라, 링컨.

그는 링컨의 얼굴 전체를 검은 두건을 당겨 덮는다.

벨 릭　　　 : 작동시켜.

바깥쪽 방에서 한 교도관이 의자의 전류를 통제하는 벽의 스위치를 내린다. 링컨은 전율한다.

4. 내부. 링컨의 감방. 아침
링컨은 엎드려 있다가 악몽으로부터 깨어난다. 그는 무기력한 상태로 숨을 몰 아쉬면서 일어나 앉는다. 천천히 그는 머리를 양손으로 감싼다.

5. 외부. 폭스 리버 교도소. 밤

6. 내부. 마이클의 감방. 아침
마이클이 세면대 옆에 앉아 있다. 그는 콘크리트의 갈라진 틈을 통해서 그 볼 트를 밀어넣는다. 밖에서 뗑그렁 소리가 나자 그는 일을 계속하기 전에 놀라 쳐다본다. 교도관이 소리를 친다.

교도관 1　　　 : (목소리) 40호 열어!

감방 문이 쓱 열리자 마이클이 벌떡 일어나 그 세면대를 원래 위치로 밀어 넣는다. 헤이와이어가 감방 밖에 나타나 걸어 들어온다. 교도관은 헤이와이어가 침대 위에 올라가자 한 쪽에 선다.

- **shudder**
  떨다, 벌벌 떨다, 몸서리 치다

- **unnerve**
  ~에게서 기력을 빼앗다, 무기력하게 하다
  - to make somebody feel nervous or frightened or lose confidence

Let's get on with it.
작동시켜.

▶ get on with는 '~을 진척시키다, 서두르다, 켜다, 지피다'의 뜻이다.

C.O. #1 : Close forty!

The door slides shut. Michael splashes his face with water from the sink and sighs before toweling himself dry.

MICHAEL : Haywire, you ever thought of breaking out?

HAYWIRE : (laughing softly) What the hell would I do out there?

MICHAEL : (dryly) Not be here.

HAYWIRE : Halfway houses. Psych visits. Meds. Checking in with a P.O. Urine tests.

Michael walks over to the door and drapes himself over the bars.

HAYWIRE : Keepin' a job. No. Why you ask?

MICHAEL : (testing him) This guy was talking about it in the yard yesterday. I didn't know what to say.

HAYWIRE : (whispering) Tell Officer Bellick. He'll make life easy for you if, uh ...

He looks up suddenly and something in Michael's tattoo catches his eye.

MICHAEL : (turning to look at him) If what?

HAYWIRE : Your tattoos.

MICHAEL : What about them?

He pulls away from the door and faces him.

교도관 1   : 40호 닫아라!

문이 미끄러지며 닫힌다. 마이클은 세면대에서 물로 얼굴을 튀기고는 수건으로 얼굴을 닦기 전에 한숨 짓는다.

마이클   : 헤이와이어, 탈옥 생각해 본 적 있어?
헤이와이어   : (부드럽게 웃으면서) 나가서 뭐하게?
마이클   : (냉담하게) 여기보다 낫잖아.
헤이와이어   : 사회 복귀 시설에, 정신 병원, 약, 가석방 담당관
                 에게 확인 받고, 소변 테스트에.

마이클은 문으로 걸어가 철창 위에 팔을 아무렇게나 얹는다.

헤이와이어   : 직장도 다녀야지. 됐어. 왜 묻는데?
마이클   : (그를 시험하면서) 어제 운동장에서 그런 얘기를 하
                 는 녀석이 있었어. 뭐라 할지 모르겠더군.
헤이와이어   : (속삭이면서) 벨릭 교도관한테 말해. 덕분에 살기
                 편해질지 몰라, 혹시…

그는 갑자기 올려다 보다가 마이클의 문신의 뭔가에 눈을 고정시킨다.

마이클   : (돌아서 그를 바라보면서) 혹시 뭐?
헤이와이어   : 네 문신 말이야.
마이클   : 그게 뭐?

그는 문에서 떨어지며 그와 마주한다.

- **halfway house**
  (만기 출소자 · 알코올 중독자 · 정신 장애자 등의) 갱생 시설

- **P.O.**
  가석방 담당관(parole officer의 약어)

- **urine**
  오줌, 소변
  - the waste liquid that collects in the bladder and that you pass from your body

- **drape**
  팔을 아무렇게나 얹다, 척 걸치다
  - to hang clothes, materials, etc. loosely on somebody/something
  - to allow part of your body to rest on something in a relaxed way

If what?

혹시 뭐라는 거야?

▶ 헤이와이어가 if … 하고는 말을 하지 않으므로 그 말을 재촉하는 표현임.

HAYWIRE : (looking him over) What are they of? No, no, no, what ... what are they? Like some kind of—

Michael reaches below Haywire's bunk to his own to get another sweatshirt.

MICHAEL : They're just tattoos.

C.O. Mack taps on the bars.

C.O. MACK : Candy time, Haywire.

Haywire hops off the bunk to take his meds and walks over to the door as Michael pulls the shirt over his head.

HAYWIRE : (turning back to Michael) They think I have schizo affective disorder with bipolar tendencies.

C.O. MACK : They think you got it?

HAYWIRE : (turning to the doc) Whatever.

He takes the pills from the doctor and throws them at the back of his throat before drinking from a cup of water. He swallows the pills at one gulf.

HAYWIRE : Ahhh.

He sticks his tongue out to the doctor.
The doctor shines a light inside, checking. The pills are gone.
Haywire turns back to Michael.

HAYWIRE : I take the pills to keep the quacks off my back.

헤이와이어 : (그를 살펴면서) 뭘 새긴 거야? 아니, 아니, 아니,
그게 뭐… 뭐야? 마치 일종의―

마이클은 헤이와이어의 침대 밑 자신의 침대에 손을 뻗쳐 다른 스웨터를 집는다.

마이클 : 그냥 문신일 뿐이야.

맥 교도관이 철창을 두드린다.

맥 교도관 : 약 먹을 시간이다, 헤이와이어.

헤이와이어는 약을 먹기 위해 침대에서 뛰어내려 문으로 가는데 그때 마이클
은 머리 위로 스웨터를 당겨 입는다.

헤이와이어 : (마이클에게 다시 돌아서며) 저 치들은 내가 양극단의
경향이 있는 정신 분열 장애라고 생각하고 있어.

맥 교도관 : 그게 맞아?

헤이와이어 : (의사에게 돌아서며) 어쨌거나.

그는 의사로부터 알약을 받아 목구멍 뒤쪽에 쏟아넣고는 한 잔의 물을 마신
다. 그는 그 알약을 한 입에 꿀꺽 삼킨다.

헤이와이어 : 아아아.

그는 자기 혓바닥을 내밀어 의사에게 보여준다.
의사는 전등으로 안을 비추며 검사한다. 알약은 사라졌다.
헤이와이어는 다시 마이클에게 돌아선다.

헤이와이어 : 잔소리 듣지 않으려고 약 먹는 거야.

■ **schizo**
〈구어〉 정신 분열증 환자

■ **affective**
감정적인, 정서적인
• affective disorder
〈정신의학〉 정서 장애

■ **bipolar**
두 극이 있는, 양극의, 상반하는, 양극
단의
- a term used to define things with
two cusually opposing poles

■ **quack**
돌팔이 의사, 시끄러운 수다떨기, 꽥꽥
우는 소리

Whatever.
어쨌거나.

▶ 한 마디로 사용하여 '무엇이든지'의 뜻으로 구어체에서 잘 쓰인다.

C.O. Mack and the doc walk off.

HAYWIRE   : Bye, now.

He pushes past Michael.

HAYWIRE   : Get out of the way.

He goes over to the toilet and bends over the sink assembly. He sticks his finger down his throat, retches, and spits out the pills.

MICHAEL   : You know, maybe they give you those things for a reason.

Haywire flushes the toilet.

HAYWIRE   : (turning back to Michael) Yeah. To keep me dull. To keep me in their invisible freakin' handcuffs. Seriously, though, those tattoos, they're beautiful.

Michael pulls out another shirt on his bunk.

HAYWIRE   : You mind if I, you know, look at the whole thing?
MICHAEL   : I do, actually.

He pulls on the other shirt.

HAYWIRE   : (confused) Why?
C.O.   : (V.O.) Yo. Stand clear.

맥 교도관과 의사가 사라진다.

헤이와이어 : 잘 가쇼.

그는 밀면서 마이클을 지나친다.

헤이와이어 : 비켜.

그는 세면대로 가서 허리를 굽힌다. 그는 손가락을 목구멍으로 집어넣고는 욕지기를 하며 알약을 뱉어낸다.

마이클 : 이유가 있어서 약을 주는 건지도 모르잖아.

헤이와이어는 세면대의 물을 내린다.

헤이와이어 : (마이클에게 돌아서며) 맞아. 날 바보로 만들려는 거야. 눈에 안 보이는 망할 족쇄를 채우려는 거지. 근데 그 문신 말이야, 정말 멋지군.

마이클은 자기 침대에서 다른 셔츠를 꺼낸다.

헤이와이어 : 그거 전부 봐도 될까?
마이클 : 사실은 싫어.

그는 다른 셔츠를 입는다.

헤이와이어 : (어리둥절해서) 왜?
교도관 : (목소리) 모두. 물러 서라.

■ **retch**
욕지기 나다
- to make sounds and movements as if you are vomiting although you do not actually do so

■ **freaking**
〈속어〉 가혹한, 호된

Get out of the way.
비켜요.

▶ get out of the way는 '피하나, 비키다'는 뜻의 관용구이다.

Michael fixes his collar.

MICHAEL   : Does there need to be a reason?

The cell door slides open. He steps outside the open cell door.
Haywire just stands there.

7. EXT. PRISON YARD. DAY
Michael walks toward Sucre, who is passing him.

MICHAEL   : Sucre—

SUCRE   : (walking past) I'm not even talkin' to you, man.

Michael turns to watch him leave, seeing Haywire staring intensely at him by the
gate. He turns around again and rolls up his sleeve to bare part of his tattoo. It says
"Cute Poison."

Flashback.

8. INT. MICHAEL'S APARTMENT. NIGHT
Michael sits at his desk, working through a pile of information. He looks up at his
wall, goes over to it and writes something on a piece of paper full of chemical
information. Over an equation he writes "Cute Poison."

End flashback.

9. EXT. PRISON YARD. DAY
Michael is looking down his arm, pondering.

ABRUZZI   : (approaching) What's the problem?

MICHAEL   : Nothing I can't handle.

ABRUZZI   : Well, I knew there was a problem. I could tell by
                 lookin' at you from across the yard. (turning to his cronies)
                 Guys, didn't I say there was a problem?

마이클은 셔츠의 깃을 고친다.

마이클 　　　: 꼭 이유가 있어야 해?

감방 문이 쓱 열린다. 그는 열린 감방 문 밖에 선다.
헤이와이어는 그냥 거기에 서 있다.

7. 외부. 교도소 운동장. 낮
마이클이 수크레를 향해 가는데 그는 마이클을 지나쳐 간다.

마이클 　　　: 수크레—
수크레 　　　: (지나가며) 너랑 할 얘기 없어.

마이클은 돌아서서 그가 가는 것을 지켜보다가 문 옆에서 자신을 열심히 응시하고 있는 헤이와이어를 본다. 그는 다시돌아 서서 문신이 노출된 부분까지 소매를 올린다. 거기에는 '짜릿한 독극물'이라고 쓰여 있다.

플래시백.

8. 내부. 마이클의 아파트. 밤
마이클은 책상에 앉아 정보의 더미를 보며 일하고 있다. 그는 벽을 쳐다보고는 거기로 걸어가 화학 지식으로 가득찬 종이 쪽지 위에 뭔가를 쓴다. 한 방정식 위에 그는 '짜릿한 독극물'이라고 쓴다.

플래시백이 끝난다.

9. 외부. 교도소 운동장. 낮
마이클은 생각에 잠겨 자기 팔을 내려다 보고 있다.

아브루치 　　　: (다가오면서) 무슨 문제라도 있나?
마이클 　　　: 문제 없어.
아브루치 　　　: 딱 보면 알아. 운동장 건너편에서 걸어오는 모습
　　　　　　　　이 그랬거든. (자기 일당에게 돌아서며) 거봐, 내가 문
　　　　　　　　제 있다고 했었지?

- **intensely**
　집중해서, 긴장해서

- **bare**
　노출된, 빈
　- not covered by any clothes

- **equation**
　〈수학, 화학〉 방정식, 등식
　- a statement showing that two
　　amounts or values are equal, for
　　example 2x + y = 54

Nothing I can't handle.
내가 해결할 수 있는 일이야.

▶ There's nothing I can't handle.이 준 표현이다.

He goes back to Michael.

ABRUZZI : So what's the problem?

Michael tilts his head in the direction of Haywire.

MICHAEL : You're lookin' at it.

Abruzzi looks at Haywire standing behind Michael.

ABRUZZI : What, Haywire?

MICHAEL : (nodding gently) Yep. He's my new cellmate.

ABRUZZI : (rolling his head, sighing) That's a problem.

MICHAEL : He doesn't sleep.

ABRUZZI : So when do you dig?

MICHAEL : (evenly) I don't.

ABRUZZI : (getting in his face) Hey, you and I are in bed now. You made me a promise. You said that we were gonna get out of here. You renege now, and I'm gonna cut you.

He claps Michael's shoulder with his hand.

ABRUZZI : So you better take care of your business, or I will take care of you.

He pulls away slightly and his tone lightens.

그는 마이클에게 돌아간다.

아브루치 : 그래 뭐가 문제야?

마이클은 자기 머리를 헤이와이어 쪽으로 까딱한다.

마이클 : 지금 보고 있잖아.

아브루치는 마이클 뒤에 서 있는 헤이와이어를 바라본다.

아브루치 : 헤이와이어 말이야?
마이클 : (부드럽게 고개를 끄덕이며) 맞아. 새로운 빵 동기인 데.
아브루치 : (머리를 굴리며, 한숨 짓고) 그게 문제야?
마이클 : 잠을 안 자거든.
아브루치 : 그럼 구멍은 언제 파?
마이클 : (차분하게) 못 파지.
아브루치 : (얼굴을 들이밀며) 이봐, 너와 난 한 배를 탄 운명이 야. 나한테 여기를 나가게 하겠다고 약속했잖아. 약속을 어겼다가는 당장 절단 날 줄 알아.

그는 마이클의 어깨를 손으로 두드린다.

아브루치 : 그러니까 제대로 처리해. 나한테 당하기 싫으면.

그는 약간 몸을 빼며 목소리가 가벼워진다.

■ **tilt**
~을 기울이다, 갸웃하다, 비스듬하게 하다
- to move, or make something move, into a position with one side or end higher than the other

■ **evenly**
차분하게, 고르게, 평탄하게, 한결같이
- calmly
- without showing any emotion
- in a smooth, regular or equal way
- with equal amounts for each person or in each place

■ **renege**
손을 떼다, 약속을 어기다
- to break a promise, an agreement, etc.

■ **clap**
~을 가볍게 두드리다, 치다
- to hit your open hands together several times to show that you approve of or have enjoyed something

You better take care of your business.
네 일을 잘처리하는 게 좋아.

▶ You had better ~ 대신 You better ~ 로 쓸때가 많음.

ABRUZZI   : Have a nice day.

He taps Michael's face and walks off. Michael watches him leave then turns back to see Haywire still standing there, watching him.

10. EXT. FOX RIVER PENITENTIARY. DAY
Camera pans over the prison.
Opening credits begin.

11. INT. POPE'S TAJ MAHAL ROOM. DAY
Michael and Pope are working before the model of the Taj Mahal.

POPE   : It's really coming together, isn't it?

Michael pops up from behind the Taj to stand beside him.

MICHAEL   : Yep.

POPE   : You think it'll be done in time?

MICHAEL   : Well, (pauses) I figure we still have the interior alcoves and pilasters to do, which is no small task. But, yes, I think so.

Pope nods in agreement.

POPE   : Listen, I have to say I ... I really appreciate all the effort that you put into this.

Michael turns away, but Pope persists.

아브루치   : 좋은 하루 보내라.

그는 마이클의 얼굴을 툭 치며 걸어간다. 마이클은 그가 가는 것을 지켜보다가
돌아서서 아직도 거기 서서 자신을 지켜보고 있는 헤이와이어를 바라본다.

10. 외부. 폭스 리버 교도소. 낮
카메라가 교도소를 비추며 내려 간다.
자막이 시작된다.

11. 내부. 포프의 타지마할 방. 낮
마이클과 포프가 타지마할의 모형 앞에서 일하고 있다.

포 프   : 제대로 돼 가는 것 같군, 안 그래?

마이클이 타지마할 뒤로부터 벌떡 일어나 그 옆에 선다.

마이클   : 네.
포 프   : 제 때 끝낼 수 있겠나?
마이클   : 글쎄요, (잠시) 아직 실내 공간과 벽기둥이 남았는
데 쉽진 않죠. 하지만 가능해요.

포프가 동의를 하며 고개를 끄덕인다.

포 프   : 이번 일 정말 이렇게 수고해줘서 뭐라 고맙다고
해야 할지.

마이클이 돌아서지만 포프는 집요하다.

- **alcove**
  반침, 벽감, 정자, 우묵한 곳, 주실에
  이어진 골방
  - an area in a room that is formed
    by part of a wall being built farther
    back than the rest of the wall

- **pilaster**
  벽면 밖으로 나오게 한 벽기둥
  - a flat column that sticks out from
    the wall of a building, used as
    decoration

Yep.
네.

▶ yep은 구어로 yes, yup 등과 같은 표현이다. 반대로 nope가 쓰인다.

POPE : Uh, I wish there was some way I could, you know, pay you or something.

MICHAEL : There is one thing you could do for me.

He pauses and turns to Pope.

MICHAEL : My cellmate.

POPE : Ah, the inimitable Charles Patoshik. Haywire.

MICHAEL : Then you know.

POPE : Hold it right there. Officer Bellick is in charge of cell transfers. You're gonna have to talk to him about that.

MICHAEL : (smiling darkly) I tried, but he seems to think we're a good match.

POPE : Has he threaten you?

MICHAEL : Who? Haywire or Bellick?

Pope takes it as a joke and laughs softly.

POPE : Unfortunately, unless there's some evidence of violence or sexual predation between cellmates, those kinds of requests fall on deaf ears around here. The prison system's a little too crowded for requests based on personality. It's not exactly sandals out there.

포 프 　 : 뭔가 보답할 방법이 있었으면 좋겠군.

마이클　 : 한 가지 있습니다.

그는 잠시 멈췄다가 포프에게 돌아선다.

마이클　 : 제 감방 동기요.

포 프 　 : 아, 헤이와이어라는 찰스 파토식 말이군.

마이클　 : 아시는군요.

포 프 　 : 그만 얘기하게. 감방 이전은 벨릭 교도관이 책임
　　　　　 지고 있어. 그 문제라면 자네가 직접 말해야 할
　　　　　 거야.

마이클　 : (어둡게 미소 지으며) 말했지만 그는 우리 둘이 잘 어
　　　　　 울린다고 생각하세요.

포 프 　 : 그가 협박하던가?

마이클　 : 누가요? 헤이와이어요, 벨릭요?

포프는 그것을 농담으로 받아들이며 부드럽게 웃는다.

포 프 　 : 불행스럽게도, 여기선 폭행이나 재소자 간 성폭
　　　　　 행 증거가 없으면 그런 요청은 무시되는 경우가
　　　　　 허다해. 성격 문제로 감방을 바꾸기엔 교도소 시
　　　　　 설이 너무 비좁거든. 입맛에 맞춰 살 수 있는 곳
　　　　　 이 아니야.

■ **inimitable**
흉내 낼 수 없는, 독특한, 추종을 불허
하는
- too good or individual for anyone
  else to copy with the same effect

■ **predation**
포식, 약탈
- the act of an animal killing and
  eating other animals

■ **fall on deaf ears**
주의를 끌지 못하다, 무시당하다, 쇠귀
에 경 읽기다

Hold it right there.
거기서 그만 하게.

▶ hold it은 구어로 '움직이지 않다, 가만 있다, 잠깐 기다리다'의 뜻이다.

There's a knock at the door. Pope's secretary, Becky, enters.

BECKY   : Warden, sorry. Your wife is here.

POPE   : What? She's not supposed to be here till four o'clock.

He walks toward her buttoning up his vest.

POPE   : Becky, do not let her come in here under any
                  circumstances. She's not supposed to see this until
                  our anniversary. I'll be right out.

He turns back to Michael and Becky leaves. Giving Michael a quick glance, he grabs his suit jacket and follows her.

12. INT. ADMIN AREA. DAY
Pope walks out from his office shrugging on his coat.

POPE   : Hi, sweetheart. You're early. Uh, let's go eat.

JUDY   : You're acting funny.

POPE   : I am?

JUDY   : (smiling) What's going on in there?

POPE   : Oh, just goin' over some files.

JUDY   : Becky said you were in a meeting.

Pope glances over at Becky and then back to Judy.

JUDY   : This isn't Toledo all over again, is it?

문에서 노크 소리가 난다. 포프의 비서인 베키가 들어온다.

베 키	: 죄송한데요, 소장님. 사모님께서 오셨어요.
포 프	: 뭐? 4시나 돼야 올 줄 알았는데.

그는 조끼의 단추를 채우면서 그녀를 향해 간다.

포 프	: 베키, 절대 여기 들여보내면 안 돼. 저건 결혼 기념일 선물이거든. 금세 나갈게.

그는 마이클에게 돌아서고 베키는 나간다. 그는 마이클을 재빨리 쳐다보고는 자신의 상의를 움켜 쥐고 그녀를 따라 나간다.

12. 내부. 행정실 부근. 낮

포프가 몸을 뒤틀며 옷을 입으면서 사무실에서 걸어 나온다.

포 프	: 안녕, 여보. 일찍 왔네. 어, 식사하러 갑시다.
주 디	: 뭔가 수상한걸요.
포 프	: 내가?
주 디	: (웃으면서) 안에 무슨 일이 있는 거죠?
포 프	: 아, 그냥 서류 좀 보고 있었어.
주 디	: 베키는 당신이 회의 중이라던데.

포프는 베키를 건너다보고 다시 주디를 돌아본다.

주 디	: 톨리도에서의 일 같은 건 아니겠죠?

- **anniversary**
(해마다 돌아오는) 기념일
- a date that is an exact number of years after the date of an important or special event

- **shrug on**
몸을 뒤틀며 (옷)을 입다

- **go over**
~을 검토하다, 점검하다, 되읽다, 복습하다
- to examine or check something carefully
- to study something carefully, especially by repeating it

Let's go eat.
식사하러 갑시다.

▶ Let's go to eat., Let's go and eat.와 같은 표현으로 go, come의 경우 to나 and를 생략할 수 있다.

POPE   : (confused and then hurts) Toledo? How can you say that?

JUDY   : Then you won't mind if I look.

She moves past him toward his office door.

POPE   : Uh, Judy ...

As he says her name, the door to Pope's office opens. Michael steps out and closes the door as Judy walks over.

MICHAEL   : Warden, I'm not going to be able to cooperate. I'd get killed if I did. Johnson's still deciding.

Pope's mouth gapes open and he recovers, realizing.

POPE   : Then you and I are done.

Michael smiles slightly and nods before walking off. Judy turns to Pope.

JUDY   : You should've just told me.

POPE   : Well, you know how anxious I get when you come around the inmates.

Judy laughs lightly.

POPE   : Becky, have a guard escort Johnson back to his cell. I'll deal with him later.

포 프　　　: (당황하고는 마음에 상처를 입는다) 톨리도? 어떻게 그렇게 말할 수 있어?

주 디　　　: 그럼 봐도 상관없겠네요?

그녀는 그 옆을 지나 사무실 문으로 향해 간다.

포 프　　　: 어, 여보…

그가 아내의 이름을 부르는데 포프의 사무실 문이 열린다. 마이클이 걸어 나와 주디가 다가갈 때 문을 닫는다.

마이클　　: 소장님, 전 협조할 수 없습니다. 그랬다간 제가 죽게 돼요. 존슨은 아직 고민 중입니다.

포프의 입이 헤벌어지다가 상황을 깨닫고 회복한다.

포 프　　　: 그럼 자네와 볼 일 끝났군.

마이클은 약하게 미소 짓고는 나가기 전에 고개를 끄덕인다. 주디는 포프에게 돌아선다.

주 디　　　: 그냥 내게 말하지 그랬어요.

포 프　　　: 당신이 수감자들 근처에 있으면 불안해서 그래.

주디는 가볍게 웃는다.

포 프　　　: 베키, 존슨은 교도관과 동행시켜. 나중에 처리할 테니까.

■ **cooperate**

협력하다, 협동하다

- to work together with somebody else in order to achieve something

■ **gape**

입을 딱 벌리다, 입을 벌리고 멍하니 바라보다

- to stare at somebody/something with your mouth open because you are shocked or surprised

You should've just told me.

그냥 나한테 말을 하지 그랬어요.

▶ I'm sorry you didn't tell me.의 의미를 내포한 표현으로 should have + p.p.는 '~해야 했다'(그런데 하지 않았다)의 뜻.

He turns back to Judy.

POPE   : Come on, let's go eat.

They exit.

13. INT. ATTORNEY/CLIENT VISITATION. DAY
Cut to a corridor. Lincoln is escorted through a door to a lawyer council room. He looks with surprise at who is standing behind a table. Shot turns around to reveal Veronica Donovan. Lincoln shuffles forward, wary.

LINCOLN   : What you doing here?

VERONICA   : I'm your attorney. I'm representing you now.

LINCOLN   : Hm.

VERONICA   : If that's all right with you.

LINCOLN   : Last time I saw you, you called me a liar.

VERONICA   : Things have changed. I believe you now.

She sits down. The door closes. Lincoln walks in and sits next to her.

VERONICA   : I got in touch with Crab Simmons' ex-girlfriend, Leticia. She corroborated your story.

LINCOLN   : (astounded) Will she testify?

VERONICA   : She's missing. I don't know, I think the Secret Service got to her.

LINCOLN   : Secret Service?

그는 다시 주디에게 돌아선다.

포 프   : 어서요, 식사하러 갑시다.

그들은 나간다.

13. 내부. 변호인 면회실. 낮

복도. 링컨은 변호인 면회실로 들어가는 문을 통해서 안내된다. 그는 테이블 뒤에 서 있는 사람을 보고 놀라서 바라본다. 카메라는 돌아서 베로니카 도노반을 비춘다. 링컨은 신중하게 발을 질질 끌며 앞으로 나온다

링 컨   : 여긴 웬 일이야?
베로니카   : 자기 변호사니까. 이제 내가 변호할 거야.
링 컨   : 음.
베로니카   : 자기만 괜찮다면.
링 컨   : 지난번 면회 땐 나더러 거짓말쟁이라더니.
베로니카   : 상황이 바뀌었어. 이젠 널 믿거든.

그녀는 앉는다. 문이 닫힌다. 링컨은 걸어 들어가 그녀 옆에 앉는다.

베로니카   : 크랩 시몬스의 애인이었던 레티샤를 만났어. 네
               말대로더군.
링 컨   : (놀라며) 그녀가 증언하겠대?
베로니카   : 그녀는 실종됐어. 모르겠어, 비밀 검찰국에 잡힌
               것 같아.
링 컨   : 비밀 검찰국?

- **attorney**
(위임장으로 정식위임 받은) 대리인, 변호사
- a lawyer, especially one who can act for somebody in a court of law

- **council**
회의, 평의회, 자문회
- (especially in the past) a formal meeting to discuss what action to take in a particular situation
- a group of people who are elected to govern an area such as a city or county

- **shuffle**
발을 질질 끌며 걷다, 발을 끌다
- to walk slowly without lifting your feet completely off the ground
- to move from one foot to another; to move your feet in an awkward or embarrassed way

- **astounded**
몹시 놀란
- very surprised or shocked by something, because it seems very unlikely

If that's all right with you.

그게 너한테 괜찮다면.

▶ If that's okay with you.와 같은 표현이다.

VERONICA : They've been pokin' around. As soon as they show up, she disappears. What do you think happened?

LINCOLN : Um, I didn't realize it was that high up, you know. Do you know what we're up against?

VERONICA : I know it's a lot more than either of us can handle on our own.

LINCOLN : (thinking) Project Justice.

VERONICA : Why have I heard of them?

LINCOLN : All they handle is death penalty cases. There's a guy there, Ben Forsik. I sent him copies of everything I had. I mean, you can go there, tell him what you found, maybe it'll be enough to bring them on board.

VERONICA : Okay.

LINCOLN : (hesitating) So, uh, how's Sebastian?

VERONICA : What do you mean?

LINCOLN : Well, you being here. I mean, is he cool with it?

VERONICA : I haven't talked to him.

Lincoln looks confused.

VERONICA : The, uh, engagement's off.

LINCOLN : Oh. Sorry. (looks down)

VERONICA : You could at least say that like you mean it.

LINCOLN : I do.

VERONICA : God, you always were a lousy liar.

베로니카	: 그들이 이리저리 쑤시고 다녔더군. 그들이 나타난 직후 그녀가 실종됐어. 어떻게 생각해?
링 컨	: 맙소사, 그렇게 높은 곳까지 관여되다니. 우리 상대가 누군지 짐작이 가?
베로니카	: 우리 힘만으론 감당할 수 없는 상대란 건 알아.
링 컨	: (생각하면서) 사법 정의 위원회.
베로니카	: 어디서 들어봤는데.
링 컨	: 사형 사건만을 다루는 곳인데. 거기 벤 포식이란 자가 있어. 내가 보낸 모든 것의 사본들을 갖고 있어. 거기 가서 알아낸 사실들을 그에게 말하면 우릴 도와줄지도 몰라.
베로니카	: 좋아.
링 컨	: (주저하면서) 근데, 저, 세바스찬은 어때?
베로니카	: 무슨 소리야?
링 컨	: 네가 여기 와서 하는 말이야. 그가 이래도 괜찮대?
베로니카	: 그에게 얘기 안 했어.

링컨은 혼란스러운 표정이다.

베로니카	: 저, 파혼했거든.
링 컨	: 저런. 유감이야. (시선을 떨군다)
베로니카	: 그냥 하는 말이면 관 둬.
링 컨	: 진심이야.
베로니카	: 넌 늘 형편없는 거짓말쟁이였잖아.

■ **poke around**
〈구어〉 뒤지다, 찾아 헤매다, 꼬치꼬치 캐다, 어슬렁거리다
- to look for something, especially something that is hidden among other things that you have to move

■ **Project Justice**
〈미〉 사법 정의 위원회(죄없는 사람들을 밝혀내고 그들의 석방을 신속히 처리하는 것이 목적임)

■ **engagement**
약혼
- an agreement to marry somebody; the period during which two people are engaged

■ **lousy**
〈구어〉 비열한, 혐오스러운, 형편없는, 저질의
- very bad
- awful
- used to show that you feel annoyed or insulted because you do not think that something is worth very much

What do you think happened?
무슨 일이 일어났다고 생각해요?

▶ Do you think?와 What happened? 두 문장이 합쳐진 표현으로 think일 경우 의문사가 문장 첫머리에 사용된다.

Lincoln nods and laughs softly.

LINCOLN : Yeah.

VERONICA : I'd better get to Project Justice.

Lincoln nods. She rises and walks away.

LINCOLN : Veronica.

She stops by the door and turns to look at him.

LINCOLN : Thank you. I didn't have a whole lot left.

VERONICA : You can thank me when I get you out of here.

Lincoln nods slightly and the door buzzes as Veronica leaves. Once she's gone, he sighs and rests his forehead on the table.

링컨은 고개를 끄덕이며 약하게 웃는다.

링 컨   : 그래.

베로니카   : 사법 정의 위원회부터 가봐야겠어.

링컨은 고개를 끄덕인다. 그녀는 일어나 나간다.

링 컨   : 베로니카.

그녀가 문간에 멈춰 서서 그를 돌아본다.

링 컨   : 고마워. 의지할 사람이 없을 줄 알았는데.

베로니카   : 고맙단 말은 네가 여기서 나가게 됐을 때 말해.

링컨은 약하게 고개를 끄덕이고 베로니카가 나가자 문에 버저가 울린다. 일단 그녀가 나가자 그는 한숨을 쉬며 테이블에 이마를 댄다.

■ **whole lot**

〈구어〉 모두, 전부

- (informal) the whole number or amount of people or things
- That's the lot.
  그게 전부다.

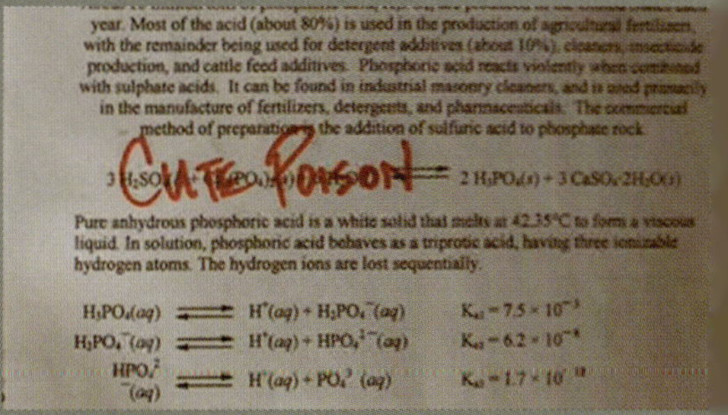

year. Most of the acid (about 80%) is used in the production of agricultural fertilizers, with the remainder being used for detergent additives (about 10%), cleaners, insecticide production, and cattle feed additives. Phosphoric acid reacts violently when combined with sulphate acids. It can be found in industrial masonry cleaners, and is used primarily in the manufacture of fertilizers, detergents, and pharmaceuticals. The commercial method of preparation is the addition of sulfuric acid to phosphate rock.

$$3\ H_2SO_4(l) + Ca_3(PO_4)_2(s) \rightleftharpoons 2\ H_3PO_4(s) + 3\ CaSO_4{\cdot}2H_2O(s)$$

Pure anhydrous phosphoric acid is a white solid that melts at 42.35°C to form a viscous liquid. In solution, phosphoric acid behaves as a triprotic acid, having three ionizable hydrogen atoms. The hydrogen ions are lost sequentially.

$$H_3PO_4(aq) \rightleftharpoons H^+(aq) + H_2PO_4^-(aq) \qquad K_{a1} = 7.5 \times 10^{-3}$$
$$H_2PO_4^-(aq) \rightleftharpoons H^+(aq) + HPO_4^{2-}(aq) \qquad K_{a2} = 6.2 \times 10^{-8}$$
$$HPO_4^{2-}(aq) \rightleftharpoons H^+(aq) + PO_4^{3-}(aq) \qquad K_{a3} = 1.7 \times 10^{-12}$$

2
자기, 난 그렇게 오래는 못 기다려
BABY, I CAN'T WAIT THAT LONG

PRISONBREAK

14. EXT. PRISON YARD. DAY
Sucre stands by the phone and calls Maricruz.

SUCRE   : Baby, it's me. Are you there? Hello? Are you there?

An inmate named ZZ, in line behind him speaks up.

ZZ   : Hey, if she is, she obviously don't want to talk to you.

Sucre gives him a look and turns back to the phone box.

SUCRE   : It's Wednesday, babe. You're gonna come around today, right? Look, I gotta hang up now. I gotta go back in the block. But you're gonna be here today, right? I'm your man, baby, and I love you. I do.

He frowns and hangs up.

15. INT. PRISON SHOWERS. DAY
Michael walks out from the communal showers with a towel wrapped around his waist. Haywire appears behind him as he picks up another towel.

HAYWIRE   : It's a pattern.

Michael spins around to look at him.

MICHAEL   : What did you say?

HAYWIRE   : Your tattoo, it's a pattern.

14. 외부. 교도소 운동장. 낮
수크레가 전화 옆에 서서 마리크루즈에게 전화를 걸고 있다.

수크레 : 자기야, 나야. 거기 있어? 여보세요? 거기 있는 거야?

지지라 불리는 수감자가 그 뒤에 줄 서 있다가 말한다.

지지 : 이봐, 안 받는 걸 보니 통화하기 싫은 것 같은데.

수크레는 그를 한번 쳐다보고는 다시 전화통으로 돌아선다.

수크레 : 오늘이 수요일이야, 자기. 오늘 올 거지? 이제 전화 끊고 감방으로 돌아가야 해. 오늘 올 거지? 자기야, 나한테는 자기 뿐이야, 그리고 사랑해. 정말 사랑해.

그는 이맛살을 찌푸리며 전화를 끊는다.

15. 내부. 교도소 샤워장. 낮
마이클이 허리 주위를 타월로 감싼 채 공동 샤워실로부터 걸어 나온다. 그가 다른 타월을 집을 때 헤이와이어가 그의 뒤에 나타난다.

헤이와이어 : 도안이군.

마이클은 빙 돌아 그를 본다.

마이클 : 뭐라고 했어?
헤이와이어 : 네 문신 말이야, 도안이라고.

■ **babe**
(사랑하는 사람에 대해) 여보, 내 사랑 (호칭), 〈속어〉귀여운 계집애, 아가씨
- a word used to address a young woman, or your wife, husband or lover, usually expressing affection but sometimes considered offensive if used by a man to a woman he does not know
- an attractive young woman

■ **come around**
돌아오다, 닥쳐 오다, 훌쩍 나타나다, 방문하다
- to come to a place, especially somebody's house, to visit for a short time

■ **frown**
눈살을 찌푸리다, 언짢은 얼굴을 하다
- to make a serious, angry or worried expression by bringing your eyebrows closer together so that lines appear on your forehead

I gotta hang up now.
이제 전화를 끊어야 해.

▶ I have to hang up now., I've got to hang up now.와 같은 표현이다.

Michael wraps the second towel around his shoulders, covering the tattoos and picking up his clothes.

MICHAEL   : You're seein' things.

He walks out, and Haywire watches him, thinking.

16. INT. POPE'S OFFICE. DAY
Bellick and Pope are in a meeting.

POPE   : Putting him in with Haywire is a low blow, Deputy.

BELLICK   : What? The shrinks cleared Haywire for reentry into Gen Pop. Besides, he's so doped up on meds he's like a kitten these days.

POPE   : (with a short laugh) A kitten who murdered both his parents.

BELLICK   : All due respect, sir, if you give Scofield preferential treatment, it'll undermine your credibility.

Pope looks to him with slight surprise.

BELLICK   : Look, I know you got a soft spot for the guy because he's got brains in his head and he's helping you with that contraption in there. But the guy's a violent criminal.

Pope begins to say something but Bellick cuts him off.

마이클은 어깨 주위에 두 번째 타월을 두르면서 문신을 가리고는 옷을 집어든다.

마이클 : 엉뚱한 상상하지 마.

그는 걸어나가는데 헤이와이어는 생각에 잠겨 그를 지켜본다.

16. 내부. 포프의 사무실. 낮
벨릭과 포프가 마주하고 있다.

포 프 : 헤이와이어와 같이 넣다니 야비한 수법이야, 부
소장.
벨 릭 : 왜요? 정신과 의사가 헤이와이어를 일반동에 다
시 넣는 데 동의한 데다 요즘 약에 취해서 얌전
한 걸요.
포 프 : (짧게 웃으며) 부모를 다 살해한 녀석이잖아.
벨 릭 : 스코필드를 편애하시면 소장님 신뢰에 악영향만
끼칩니다.

포프는 약간 놀라서 그를 응시한다.

벨 릭 : 그 녀석이 머리도 있고 소장님이 그 고안물 만드
는 일을 도와준다고 잘 보셨나 본데요. 하지만
녀석은 중범죄자입니다.

포프는 뭔가 말하기를 시작하는데 벨릭이 말을 막는다.

■ **deputy**
대리인, 부소장, 대리역

■ **shrink**
〈속어〉정신과 의사
- a psychiatrist or psychologist

■ **credibility**
신용, 믿을 수 있음, 신빙성

■ **contraption**
〈구어〉새 고안물, 기묘한 장치
- a machine or piece of equipment
  that looks strange

He's so doped up on meds.
그는 약에 취해 있다.

▶ dope up은 속어로 '마약으로 기분이 좋아지다, 마약을 복용하다'의 관용어이다.

BELLICK : He deserves punishment just as much as the rest of these guys.

POPE : (nodding but pushing it aside) You have been here long enough to know that I'm less interested in punishment than I am in rehabilitation. And sticking him in with Haywire is not rehabilitation in my book.

BELLICK : (removing his cap) You delegated authority over Gen Pop to me, boss.

POPE : I know I did.

BELLICK : Well then, you either gotta let me do my job or pass it onto somebody else.

POPE : Now, Brad, go easy. There's a reason I'm giving you more and more responsibility.

He moves closer to Bellick.

POPE : When I retire, I'm recommending you to take my place. Don't make me regret it.

Bellick is surprised.

POPE : All I'm saying is take another look at the Scofield situation. I trust your judgment.

BELLICK : (nodding) Yes, sir.

He walks off.

벨 릭　：다른 죄수들처럼 그 녀석도 처벌을 받아야 한다
　　　　고요.

포 프　：*(고개를 끄덕이지만 그 말을 무시하며)* 그만큼 오래 있었
　　　　으면 내가 처벌보다 교화에 더 관심이 있다는 거
　　　　알 거네. 그리고 그를 헤이와이어와 한 방을 쓰
　　　　게 한 건 교화가 아니야.

벨 릭　：*(모자를 벗으면서)* 일반 감방에 대한 권한은 제게 맡
　　　　기셨잖아요, 소장님.

포 프　：알아.

벨 릭　：그럼 제가 알아서 하게 두시든가 아니면 다른 사
　　　　람한테 넘기든가 하시죠.

포 프　：이보게, 브래드, 살살 하라는 뜻이야. 자네한테
　　　　책임을 더 많이 부여하는 데는 이유가 있어.

그는 벨릭에게 더 가까이 다가간다.

포 프　：내가 은퇴하게 되면 자네를 내 후임자로 추천할
　　　　거야. 그 결정을 후회하지 않게 해주게.

벨릭은 놀란다.

포 프　：스코필드의 상황을 재검토해 봐. 자네 판단을 믿
　　　　겠네.

벨 릭　：*(고개를 끄덕이며)* 알겠습니다.

그는 걸어나간다.

■ **rehabilitation**
(장애자 등의) 사회 복귀, 갱생, 명예
회복
  • rehabilitate
    ~의 명예를 회복시키다, 사회 복귀
    시키다
    - to help somebody to have a
      normal, useful life again after
      they have been very ill/sick or in
      prison for a long time

■ **delegate**
(권한 등을) 위임하다
  - to give part of your work, power or
    authority to somebody in a lower
    position than you
  - to choose somebody to do
    something

I'm recommending you to take my place.
자네를 내 후임자로 추천할 거야.

▶ take one's place는 '~의 자리를 차지하다, 대신하다'의 뜻이다.

17. INT. CLOSED VISITATION AREA. DAY

The inmates walk into the open visiting area. Sucre walks down the line to the main room but gets the door shut in his face by C.O. Mack.

SUCRE : Whoa, whoa, whoa, wait. What's up? This is supposed to be an open visitation. Why we doin' it here?

C.O. MACK : Ask your visitor.

Sucre turns to look at who's visiting him in a segregated area. Hector stands there. He walks up to Hector.

SUCRE : What are you doin' here? Where's Maricruz?

They sit down.

HECTOR : She's not gonna be comin' around here anymore.

SUCRE : Is she hurt?

HECTOR : No, no. She's fine, she's fine. She just, uh ... (pauses) She's with me now.

SUCRE : She's with you now?

He smiles, looking around.

SUCRE : This is a joke, right?

HECTOR : She made a decision, man. She decided she needed stability.

SUCRE : (disbelievingly) Is she gonna get that from you?

17. 내부. 밀폐된 면회 지역. 낮

수감자들이 공개 면회 지역으로 걸어 들어간다. 수크레가 줄을 따라 면회실로 걸어가지만 맥 교도관이 수크레 앞에서 문을 닫아버린다.

수크레	: 와, 와, 와, 기다려요. 공개 면회인데 왜 이러는 겁니까?
맥 교도관	: 면회인한테 물어봐.

수크레는 분리된 지역에서 자신을 방문하고 있는 사람을 보기 위해 돌아선다. 헥터가 거기 서 있다. 그는 헥터에게 걸어간다.

수크레	: 네 놈이 여기서 뭐 하는 거야? 마리는 어디 있어?

그들은 앉는다.

헥 터	: 그녀는 더는 여기 안 올 거야.
수크레	: 어디 다쳤어?
헥 터	: 아니, 무사해. 잘 있어, 잘 있어. 그냥… 저… (잠시) 지금은 나와 함께 있거든.
수크레	: 지금 너랑 있다니?

그는 웃으며 주위를 둘러본다.

수크레	: 농담이지?
헥 터	: 그녀가 내린 결정이야. 안정된 생활이 필요하니까.
수크레	: (믿을 수 없다는 듯이) 너한테서 안정을 찾는다고?

■ **segregated**
격리된, 분리된
- segregate
  분리하다, 격리하다
  - to separate people of different races, religions or sexes and treat them differently

■ **stability**
안정, 확고, 안정성
- the quality or state of being steady and not changing or being disturbed in any way (= the quality of being stable)

She's not gonna be comin' around here anymore.

그녀는 더는 여기 안 올 거야.

▶ come, go, start, leave, arrive등과 같은 동사는 진행형으로 '미래'를 나타내기도 한다.

HECTOR : Look, you can think whatever you want about me. But, uh, ...

He taps on the glass.

HECTOR : ... I'm not the one who's in prison. See, I actually can do something for her. And she wanted me to stop by here and talk to you first, you know, in case you got mad—

Sucre stands up and bangs on the glass shouting in Spanish at him. Hector stands back and a C.O. comes in to restrain Sucre. Sucre steps back, hands up quietly.

HECTOR : You just proved my point. You're a con, and that's all you'll ever be.

Sucre kisses his fist and points at him angrily. It means a threatening gesture to Hector. Hector stares scoffing and then walks off. Sucre's head drops dejectedly.

18. EXT. TOXIC CONTROL CENTER. DAY
The sign "Toxic Control Center" is seen on the front wall of a building.

19. INT. TOXIC CONTROL CENTER. DAY
Michael walks in alone and tosses a large carton of cigarettes to the inmate at the desk.

CHOPPY : Make it quick.

Michael walks down rows of equipment, stopping in front of the masonry section. He selects a bottle of something and checks his wrist. On it is written "Cute Poison." The "CuSo" and "PO" in both words highlight. He grabs a bottle of drain cleaner and drops it in a sock stuffed up his sleeve.

헥 터　　　　： 이봐, 나에 대해 마음대로 생각해. 하지만…

그는 유리를 두드린다.

헥 터　　　　： …난 누구처럼 교도소에 있는 게 아니니까. 난 그
　　　　　　　녀에게 뭐든 해 줄 수 있거든. 나더러 여기 들러서
　　　　　　　네게 먼저 말하라더군. 네가 성낼 경우를 생각해—

수크레는 일어서서 그에게 스페인어로 소리를 지르며 유리를 탕탕 친다. 헥터
는 뒤로 일어서며 교도관이 수크레를 진정시키려 다가온다. 수크레는 뒤로 물
러 서며 조용히 손을 든다.

헥 터　　　　： 내 말이 맞잖아. 넌 전과자야, 평생 그 꼴일 거고.

수크레는 자기 주먹에 키스를 하고는 화가 나서 그를 가리킨다. 헥터에게 위
협을 주려는 의미이다. 헥터는 조소하면서 응시를 하다가 나간다. 수크레의
머리는 맥없이 떨어진다.

18. 외부. 독극물 통제 구역. 낮
'독극물 통제 구역'이란 간판이 건물 전면 벽에서 보인다.

19. 내부. 독극물 통제 구역. 낮
마이클이 혼자 걸어 들어와 책상에 앉아 있는 수감자에게 커다란 담배 꾸러미
를 던진다.

초 피　　　　： 빨리 해.

마이클은 설비물이 있는 줄을 걸어 내려가 석조용 약품부 앞에 선다. 그는 어
떤 병을 골라 자신의 손목과 대조한다. 그 위에는 '짜릿한 독극물'이라 씌어 있
다. '황산 구리'와 '인산'이란 단어들이 눈에 띈다. 그는 하수구 청소 병을 집어
들고는 자기 소매에 쑤셔 넣어진 양말에다 넣는다.

■ **restrain**
구속하다, 억제하다, 누르다
- to stop somebody/something from
  doing something, especially by
  using physical force : to stop
  yourself from feeling an emotion or
  doing something that you would
  like to do

■ **dejectedly**
맥없이, 낙심하여
- dejected
  - unhappy and disappointed

■ **masonry**
석공술, 석조 건물, 벽돌 쌓기
- the parts of a building that are
  made of stone

■ **drain**
배수로, 하수구
- a pipe that carries away dirty
  water or other liquid waste
- (*Am E* grate, sewer grate) a frame
  of metal bars over the opening to
  a drain in the ground

in case you got mad
네가 성낼 경우를 생각하여

▶ in case (that) 는 접속사 역할을 하면서 '~할 경우를 생각하여, 만일 ~라면'의 뜻이다.

CHOPPY   : (V.O., louder than necessary) Yeah. He's, uh, right in here.

BELLICK   : Take a walk, Choppy.

Bellick walks up the isle where Michael is still standing.

BELLICK   : Scofield. You're in a restricted area.

MICHAEL   : I'm doing yard work for P.I. We need some fertilizer.

BELLICK   : Then why are you in the masonry section?

He draws his billy stick and approaches Michael. Michael spreads his arms. Bellick searches through his jacket with the stick. He doesn't find the bottle. He pulls away.

BELLICK   : Oh, by the way, how's the foot?

He stomps the heel of his boot hard onto Michael's toe stumps. Michael groans hard and doubles over in pain. Bellick puts a hand on his shoulder and twists his heel, grinding the end of his boot harder into the toes of Michael's work boots. Michael collapses, breathing heavily. He grabs a hold of his foot in agony. Bellick squats down beside him.

BELLICK   : Don't ever go around me to the Pope again. (stands up) Now, move.

Tentatively, Michael stands up and walks as steadily as he can toward the door. The shot runs through the tunnels of the prison.

20. INT. MICHAEL'S CELL. DAY
The next day. Michael spits out water after brushing his teeth. He thinks a while and looks up.

초 피   : (목소리. 필요 이상으로 크게) 네. 그는 여기 있습니다.

벨 릭   : 나가 있어, 초피.

벨릭은 아직 마이클이 서 있는 통로로 걸어온다.

벨 릭   : 스코필드. 여긴 제한 구역일 텐데.

마이클   : 교도소 사업으로 운동장에 쓸 비료가 필요해서요.

벨 릭   : 근데 왜 석조용 약품 구역에 있나?

그는 자신의 곤봉을 꺼내 마이클에게 다가온다. 마이클은 팔을 펼친다. 벨릭은 곤봉으로 상의 전체를 수색한다. 그는 병을 찾아내지 못한다. 그는 물러 선다.

벨 릭   : 아, 그런데, 발은 어때?

그는 자신의 부츠 뒤꿈치로 마이클의 발가락 그루터기 위를 짓밟는다. 마이클은 몹시 신음을 하며 고통스러워 몸을 구부린다. 벨릭은 그의 어깨 위에 한 손을 올려 놓고 자기 발꿈치를 비틀며 마이클의 작업화 발가락에다 자신의 부츠 끝부분을 갈아댄다. 마이클은 헐떡거리면서 쓰러진다. 그는 고뇌하면서 자기 발을 움켜쥔다. 벨릭은 그 옆에 쭈그려 앉는다.

벨 릭   : 다시는 소장한테 헛소리 까발리지 마. (일어선다)
          그만 꺼져.

시험 삼아, 마이클은 일어서서 문을 향해 될 수 있는 한 견실하게 걸어 본다. 카메라는 교도소의 터널을 통해 달려간다.

20. 내부. 마이클의 감방. 낮
다음 날, 마이클은 이를 닦은 후에 물을 뱉어낸다. 그는 잠시 생각을 하고는 쳐다본다.

- **billy**
  〈구어〉 곤봉, 경찰봉

- **stump**
  그루터기, (손발의) 잘리고 남은 부분, 기부
  - the bottom part of a tree left in the ground after the rest has fallen or been cut down
  - the end of something or the part that is left after the main part has been cut, broken off or worn away

- **double over**
  (고통으로) 몸을 구부리다
  - to bend or to make your body bend over quickly, for example because you are in pain

- **tentatively**
  시험적으로, 시험 삼아, 주저하면서

- **steadily**
  견실하게, 착실하게, 끊임없이

By the way, how's the foot?
그런데, 발은 어때?

▶ by the way는 '그런데, 말이 난 김에, 도중에'의 뜻으로 화제를 바꾸면서 사용하는 표현이다.

MICHAEL   : You know what, Haywire? I don't think we're gonna work out.

He turns around to look at Haywire.

MICHAEL   : And since I was here first, I think you should go.

Shot swings around to Haywire, sitting on his bed, clutching his pillow.

HAYWIRE   : I crapped myself once in junior high.

Michael looks mildly frustrated.

HAYWIRE   : During ... during P.E., we were playing badminton, ...

Michael looks down at the sink, where Haywire has his toiletries anally organized.

HAYWIRE   : ... and I knew I was gonna have to walk past a bunch of the other students to, you know, get back to the locker room, ...

Michael picks up Haywire's tube of the toothpaste. He unscrews the cap and squeezes it out, directing the flow into the toilet.

HAYWIRE   : ... and so I just started walking ... And I tried to make fun of it, you know, before anyone else did. So I turned around behind me, and I said, "Look, I have a tail."

마이클 　: 그거 알아, 헤이와이어? 아무래도 우린 잘 지내
　　　　　 지 못할 것 같아.

그는 돌아서서 헤이와이어를 바라본다.

마이클 　: 여기 내가 먼저 왔으니까 네가 나가줘야겠어.

카메라는 빙 돌아 침대 위에 앉아 베개를 움켜 쥐고 있는 헤이와이어를 비춘다.

헤이와이어 　: 중학교 때 바지에 똥을 싼 적이 있었어.

마이클은 다소 좌절에 빠진 표정이다.

헤이와이어 　: 체육 시간이었는데 우린 배드민턴을 치고 있었지…

마이클은 세면대를 내려다 본다. 거기에는 헤이와이어의 화장품류가 지나치게 꼼꼼하게 정돈되어 있다.

헤이와이어 　: …사물함으로 가려면 애들 앞으로 지나가야 한다
　　　　　　 는 걸 알고 있었지, …

마이클은 헤이와이어의 치약 튜브를 집어든다. 그는 뚜껑을 열고는 치약을 다 짜서 변기 속으로 다 흘려버린다.

헤이와이어 　: …그래서 천천히 걷기 시작했지… 딴 애가 그걸
　　　　　　 놀림감으로 삼기 전에 선수를 치기로 했어. 그
　　　　　　 래서 뒤로 돌아서서 "이봐, 내게 꼬리가 생겼다"
　　　　　　 고 말했지.

- **clutch**
　~을 꽉 잡다, 움켜 쥐다
　- to hold somebody/something
　　tightly
　- to take hold of something suddenly,
　　because you are afraid or in pain

- **crap**
　〈비어〉 배변하다

- **mildly**
　다소, 약간
　- slightly
　- not very much
　- in a gentle manner

- **toiletry**
　화장품류(비누, 치약 등 세면용품 포함)

- **anally**
　〈구어〉 (지나치게) 꼼꼼하게, 까다롭게

I tried to make fun of it.

난 그걸 놀림감으로 삼으려 했다.

▶ make fun of는 '~을 놀리다, 조소하다, 놀림감으로 삼다'의 뜻이다.

He laughs. Michael puts the empty tube into his pocket and flushes the toilet.
Haywire leans over the edge of the bed, where Michael's head is, waiting anxiously.

HAYWIRE : I just shared a secret with you. (whispers) Now it's your turn.

MICHAEL : You wanna know what the tattoos mean?

HAYWIRE : (excited) Yeah.

MICHAEL : (shortly) Nothing.

He walks off. Haywire looks confused that his plan didn't work. Michael walks to the cell door.
Abruzzi walks up.

ABRUZZI : Hey, fish. Making any progress?

MICHAEL : (leaning his head on the wall) With Sleeping Beauty back there, or with the digging?

ABRUZZI : Either.

MICHAEL : No. But I know what to do.

ABRUZZI : Oh, yeah? Problem is, you don't got the stugods to do it.

Michael looks at him, he's right.

C.O. : (V.O.) Abruzzi, let's go.

ABRUZZI : See ya.

He continues walking.

그는 웃는다. 마이클은 빈 치약통을 자기 주머니에 넣고는 변기의 물을 내린다.
헤이와이어는 마이클의 머리가 있는 침대 가장자리에 기대고서 열망하며 기다
린다.

헤이와이어	: 이건 누구한테도 하지 않은 비밀이야. (속삭인다) 이제 네 차례다.
마이클	: 문신의 의미를 알고 싶어?
헤이와이어	: (흥분해서) 그래.
마이클	: (짧게) 아무 의미 없어.

그는 걸어간다. 헤이와이어는 자신의 계획이 수포로 돌아가 당황스러운 표정
이다. 마이클은 감방 문으로 간다.
아브루치가 다가온다.

아브루치	: 이봐, 신참. 진척은 좀 있나?
마이클	: (벽에 머리를 기대면서) 잠 자는 숲 속의 미녀 일, 아니면 구멍 파는 일?
아브루치	: 둘 다.
마이클	: 전혀. 하지만 방법은 알아.
아브루치	: 그래? 문제는 네게 그럴 배짱이 없다는 거겠지.

마이클은 그를 바라본다. 그의 말이 옳다.

교도관	: (목소리) 아브루치, 가자.
아브루치	: 또 보자고.

그는 계속 걸어간다.

- **anxiously**
  열망하여, 근심스럽게
  - anxious
    - feeling worried or nervous
    - causing anxiety
    - showing anxiety

- **Sleeping Beauty**
  잠자는 미녀 (늙은 마녀의 마술로 백년
  동안 잠잔 아름다운 공주), 의식 없는
  사람(여기서는 Haywire를 가리킴)

- **stugods**
  〈속어〉 용기, 만용

Making any progress?
진척은 좀 있나?

▶ Are you making any progress?의 준말로 make progress는 '진행하다, 전진하다,
진보하다, 향상하다'의 뜻임.

21. EXT. PRISON YARD. DAY
ZZ's using the phone.

ZZ : (on the phone) Yeah? Really? Well, tell the crazy son of a bitch I said hi.

Sucre hurries over to him.

SUCRE : (gesturing) Wrap it up.

ZZ : (on the phone) How about Aunt Ruth? She out of the hospital yet?

SUCRE : Wrap it up.

ZZ : Hold on, Ma.

He puts his hand around the phone.

ZZ : (to Sucre) Bite me.

Sucre reaches out and slams the connection line down. ZZ drops the receiver, pissed.

ZZ : Okay, we got a problem now, man.

SUCRE : (getting into his face) Let's handle it then.

ZZ laughs, doesn't think it's worth the effort and walks off.

SUCRE : Just what I thought.

He reaches out to take the phone and dials a number.

21. 외부. 교도소 운동장. 낮
지지가 전화를 쓰고 있다.

지 지   : (전화로) 예? 정말요? 그럼, 그 미친 놈한테 안부 전해 주세요.

수크레가 그에게 급히 다가온다.

수크레   : (몸짓을 하며) 그만 끊어.

지 지   : (전화로) 루스 숙모는 어떠세요? 퇴원하셨나요?

수크레   : 끊으라니까.

지 지   : 잠깐만, 엄마.

그는 전화기 주위에 손을 놓는다.

지 지   : (수크레에게) 건드리지 마.

수크레는 손을 뻗어 전화를 쾅 끊어버린다. 지지는 화가 나서 수화기를 떨어뜨린다.

지 지   : 좋아, 이러면 곤란하지.

수크레   : (얼굴을 밀어대며) 그럼 해결 보자고.

지지는 웃으면서 더 애쓸 가치가 없다고 생각하고는 사라진다.

수크레   : 그럴 줄 알았어.

그는 손을 내밀어 수화기를 잡고는 다이얼을 돌린다.

- **wrap up**
  매듭짓다, 끝내다, 싸다
  - to complete something such as an agreement or a meeting in a satisfactory way

- **pissed**
  〈속어, 비어〉 화난, 곤드레만드레 취한
  - drunk
  - very angry or annoyed

- **It's worth the effort.**
  그건 애쓸 가치가 있다.
  worth 다음에는 명사나 동명사형이 온다.

Bite me.
건드리지 마.

▶ You bite me.로 bite는 '화나게 하다, 괴롭히다, 신경질 나게 하다'의 뜻이다

22. EXT. PARK. DAY
Maricruz answers walking in the park.

MARICRUZ : (on the cell phone) Hello.

Intercut between Sucre and Maricruz.

23. EXT. PRISON YARD. DAY

SUCRE : Maricruz? It's me, baby. What the hell is going on?

24. EXT. PARK. DAY

SUCRE : (V.O.) What's the deal with you and Hector?

MARICRUZ : When were you gonna tell me?

SUCRE : (V.O.) Tell you what?

MARICRUZ : That Rita Saldana's been visiting you.

25. EXT. PRISON YARD. DAY

SUCRE : What?

MARICRUZ : (V.O.) Yeah. Hector told me.

SUCRE : (getting angry) Hector told you ... Hector told you. Of course he told you. Baby, that guy's a snake. He's a liar.

26. EXT. PARK. DAY

22. 외부. 공원. 낮
마리크루즈가 공원을 거닐면서 전화를 받는다.

마리크루즈　：(휴대전화기로) **여보세요?**

카메라는 수크레와 마리크루즈 사이를 번갈아 비춘다.

23. 외부. 교도소 운동장. 낮

수크레　：마리크루즈? 나야, 자기. 도대체 무슨 일이야?

24. 외부. 공원. 낮

수크레　：(목소리) 너와 헥터가 어쩐다고?
마리크루즈　：내게 언제 말하려 한 거지?
수크레　：(목소리) 네게 뭘 말하려 했단 거야?
마리크루즈　：리타 살다나가 널 면회왔었단 얘기.

25. 외부. 교도소 운동장. 낮

수크레　：뭐?
마리크루즈　：그래. 헥터가 말했어.
수크레　：(화를 내며) 헥터가 말했다고… 헥터가 말했다고.
　　　　　　물론 그 자식이 말했겠지. 자기, 그 놈은 음흉한
　　　　　　인간이야. 그 자식이 거짓말 한 거야.

26. 외부. 공원. 낮

■ **deal**
(쌍방에 이익이 되는) 협정, 뒷거래, 담합
- an agreement, especially in business, on particular conditions for buying or doing something

■ **snake**
음흉한 인간, 뱀 같은 인간
- a person who pretends to be your friend but who cannot be trusted

---

Tell you what?
네게 뭘 말하려 했단 거야?

▶ 앞의 질문을 되받아 하는 말로 Was I gonna tell you what?가 준 표현이다.

MARICRUZ   : Why would he lie?

SUCRE   : (V.O.) Why would he lie?

27. EXT. PRISON YARD. DAY

SUCRE   : Because he's been trying to get into your pants since
              the minute we started dating, that's why.

28. EXT. PARK. DAY

MARICRUZ   : You know what? I don't know what to believe.

29. EXT. PRISON YARD. DAY

SUCRE   : Me, Mommy. Believe me.

MARICRUZ   : (V.O.) Yeah, while I wait by the phone twice a week.

SUCRE   : (pleading) Baby, where's this coming from?

30. EXT. PARK. DAY

MARICRUZ   : I don't know.

She sighs.

MARICRUZ   : Look, there's just so many things. Yesterday I went
              to Teresa's house and I saw her baby.

마리크루즈   : 왜 그가 거짓말을 해?
수크레   : (목소리) 왜 그가 거짓말을 하냐고?

27. 외부. 교도소 운동장. 낮

수크레   : 우리가 연애할 때부터 너와 잠자리를 같이 하려고 노려왔었어, 그게 이유야.

28. 외부. 공원. 낮

마리크루즈   : 그거 알아? 뭘 믿어야 할지 모르겠어.

29. 외부. 교도소 운동장. 낮

수크레   : 나지. 날 믿어.
마리크루즈   : (목소리) 그럼, 일주일에 두 번씩 전화하나 보고.
수크레   : (간청하면서) 자기야, 대체 왜 이러는 거야?

30. 외부. 공원. 낮

마리크루즈   : 모르겠어.

그녀는 한숨을 짓는다.

마리크루즈   : 그냥 일이 복잡해. 어제 테레사 집에 갔다가 아기를 봤어.

■ **pants**
여자용 팬티, 바지
- a piece of underwear worn by men or women under trousers/pants, a skirt, etc.

■ **the minute**
~와 동시에, ~하자마자
- as soon as

■ **pleading**
탄원하는, 변론하는
- asking somebody for something in a very strong and serious way
  • plead
    변론하다, 탄원하다

You know what?
있잖아.

▶ 말을 시작하면서 하는 표현으로 '그거 알아? 있잖아, 저 그게' 등의 뜻이다.

31. EXT. PRISON YARD. DAY

SUCRE : (laughs) Is that what this is about? You think your clock is ticking?

32. EXT. PARK. DAY

MARICRUZ : Well, I am going to be thirty in a few years.

33. EXT. PRISON YARD. DAY

SUCRE : (trying to reason with her) Baby, you're twenty-five. You wanna get pregnant, let's get pregnant right now.

34. EXT. PARK. DAY

MARICRUZ : Baby, you know I can't get pregnant till I marry you.

35. EXT. PRISON YARD. DAY

SUCRE : We're gonna get married in sixteen months.

36. EXT. PARK. DAY

MARICRUZ : Yeah, well, Hector says that if something goes wrong in there that you could serve your full sentence.

31. 외부. 교도소 운동장. 낮

수크레   : (웃는다) 이게 다 그것 때문이야? 나이 들어서 조급해서?

32. 외부. 공원. 낮

마리크루즈   : 몇 년 있으면 나도 서른이야.

33. 외부. 교도소 운동장. 낮

수크레   : (그녀를 설득하려고 애를 쓰며) 자기야, 이제 스물다섯이잖아. 아기 갖고 싶어? 지금 당장 애를 갖자고.

34. 외부. 공원. 낮

마리크루즈   : 결혼 전에는 임신할 수 없는 거 알면서.

35. 외부. 교도소 운동장. 낮

수크레   : 우린 16개월 후에 결혼할 거잖아.

36. 외부. 공원. 낮

마리크루즈   : 그래, 그런데 헥터 말이 거기서 일이 잘못되면 형기를 다 채울 수도 있다던걸.

■ **tick**

(시계 등이) 똑딱〔째깍〕거리다, (시간이) 똑딱거리며 지나가다

- (of a clock, etc.) to make short, light, regular repeated sounds to mark time passing

■ **reason with**

~을 설득하다, 설명하다, 이치를 따지다

- to talk to somebody in order to persuade them to be more sensible

■ **pregnant**

임신한

- (of a woman or female animal) having a baby or young animal developing inside her/its body

You could serve your full sentence.

넌 형기를 다 채울 수도 있어.

▶ sentence는 '형벌, 처벌, (형사상의) 판결, 선고'의 뜻이고, serve one's sentence는 '복역하다, 징역을 치르다'의 뜻임.

37. EXT. PRISON YARD. DAY

MARICRUZ : (V.O., upset) I can't wait ten years. I can't wait ten years, baby.

SUCRE : (calmly) I'm gonna be out in sixteen months. (in Spanish) Te yo prometo, mi amor.

MARICRUZ : (V.O.) Well, what if something does happen, huh?

38. EXT. PARK. DAY

MARICRUZ : Baby, I can't wait that long.

Hector walks up behind her.

MARICRUZ : I can't.

She notices him.

MARICRUZ : I'm sorry. I gotta go.

She hangs up the phone.

39. EXT. PRISON YARD. DAY

SUCRE : Hello? Wait. Hello?

He tries to connect the call again but slams the phone down.
He is restless.

37. 외부. 교도소 운동장. 낮

마리크루즈 : (목소리. 혼란에 빠져) 10년은 못 기다려. 10년은 못 기다려.

수크레 : (침착하게) 16개월 후에 출옥할 거야. (스페인어로) 자기야, 내가 약속해.

마리크루즈 : (목소리) 그러다 무슨 일이라도 생기면 어쩌지?

38. 외부. 공원. 낮

마리크루즈 : 자기, 난 그렇게 오래는 못 기다려.

헥터가 그녀 뒤에 다가온다.

마리크루즈 : 난 못해.

그녀가 그를 본다.

마리크루즈 : 미안해. 끊어야겠어.

그녀는 전화를 끊는다.

39. 외부. 교도소 운동장. 낮

수크레 : 여보세요? 잠깐만. 여보세요?

그는 다시 전화를 연결하려 하나 전화기를 쾅 하고 내려 놓는다. 그는 불안하다.

■ **Te yo prometo, mi amor.**
자기야, 내가 약속해.
영어로 I promise to you, my love. 의 뜻이다.

■ **restless**
침착하지 못한, 들떠 있는, 쉬지 못하게 하는
- unable to stay still or be happy where you are, because you are bored or need a change
- without real rest or sleep

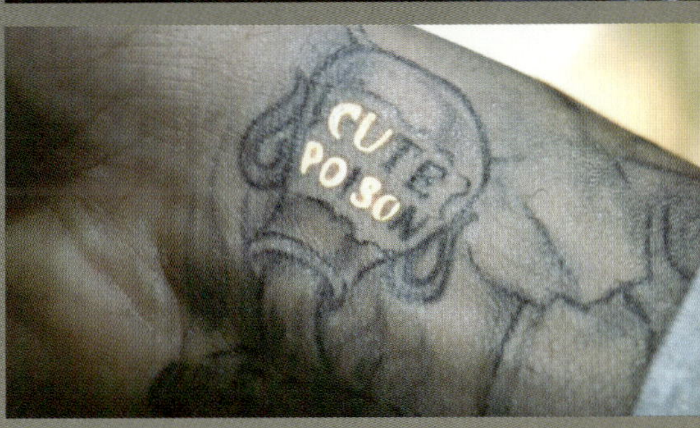

and
armaceuticals.
ric acid to phosphate rock.

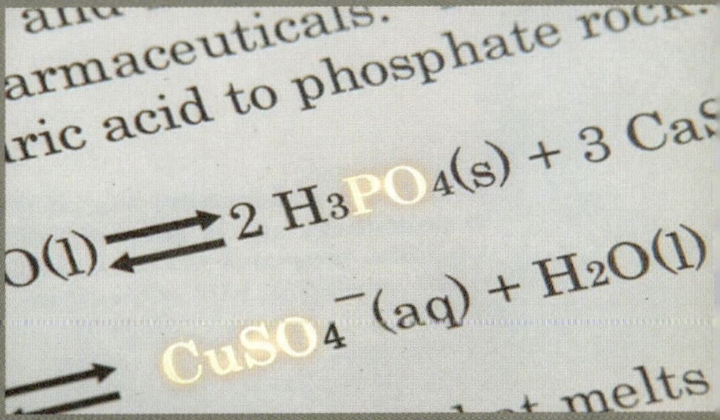

$$O(l) \rightleftharpoons 2\ H_3PO_4(s) + 3\ CaS$$

$$CuSO_4{}^-(aq) + H_2O(l)$$

$$CuSO_4$$

melts

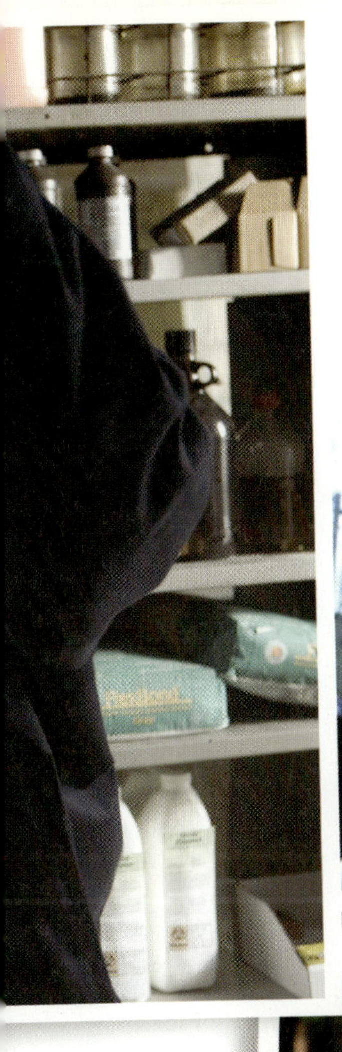

3

IF HE WAS SET UP, THEN WHY?

PRISONBREAK

40. EXT. CHICAGO. DAY
The shot pans over Chicago.

41. INT. PROJECT JUSTICE OFFICE. DAY
The shot goes to the title on the door. Project Justice. Veronica talks with Ben Forsik, one being the man Lincoln recommended. His associate, Nick, stands by the window.

BEN : Even if Leticia Barris turned up again, her testimony would be worthless. By and large, most junkies with criminal records don't shine on the stand.

VERONICA : Maybe. But I just found all this out in the past couple of days. I'm confident that I can find out a whole lot more now that I'm devoting all my time to the case.

NICK : The Secret Service agent who came to visit you when Leticia was in your office—what did he want?

BEN : Nick, please. You've gotta understand, Ms. Donovan, unless there's new information you can provide for us, we've already reviewed Mr. Burrows' case thoroughly. Do you have any new evidence?

VERONICA : No, but I—

BEN : But that's effectively what you're telling us, right? I need to clarify here.

VERONICA : Yes, that's what I'm telling you. But look, Mr. Forsik, you don't need to point out what I don't have. I am well aware of that.

Nick nods.

40. 외부. 시카고. 낮
카메라가 시카고를 비춘다.

41. 내부. 사법 정의 위원회 사무실. 낮
카메라가 문 위에 있는 글자에 간다. '사법 정의 위원회'. 베로니카는 링컨이 추천한 사람인 벤 포식에게 말을 한다. 그의 동료인 닉이 창가에 서 있다.

벤	: 레티샤 배리스가 증언한다 해도 소용 없는 일입니다. 대체로, 전과 있는 마약 중독자는 증언의 신뢰성이 떨어져요.
베로니카	: 그럴지도 모르죠. 하지만 지난 이틀간 이 정도 알아냈으니까 이 사건에 매달린다면 훨씬 더 많은 걸 알아낼 수 있을 겁니다.
닉	: 레티샤가 당신 사무실에 갔을 때 찾아왔던 비밀 검찰국 요원이 원하던 게 뭐였죠?
벤	: 닉, 그만 하게. 도노반 양, 새로운 증거를 제시하지 않는 한 버로스 씨 사건은 이미 재검토를 끝낸 상태입니다. 새로운 증거가 있나요?
베로니카	: 아니요, 하지만—
벤	: 하지만 사실은 없는 거죠? 분명히 할 필요가 있습니다.
베로니카	: 네, 그게 사실입니다. 하지만 포식 씨, 그건 지적하실 필요 없어요. 그건 잘 알고 있으니까.

닉이 고개를 끄덕인다.

- **by and large**
  전반적으로, 대체로
  - used when you are saying something that is generally, but not completely true

- **junkie**
  〈속어〉 아편쟁이, 마약 중독자
  - a drug addict (= a person who is unable to stop taking dangerous drugs)

- **thoroughly**
  철저히, 완전히
  - very much
  - completely
  - completely and with great attention to detail

- **clarify**
  명백하게 하다, 뚜렷하게 하다
  - to make something clearer or easier to understand

I am well aware of that.
그건 잘 알고 있다.

▶ I know that well.의 뜻으로 be aware of는 '~을 알아채다, 알다'의 의미다.

VERONICA : I'm here asking for your help because I don't think an innocent man should be killed for something he didn't do. And I believe that's what it says on your mission statement in the lobby.

BEN : (not unkindly) We get thousands of requests for representation.

VERONICA : (quickly) I'm sure you do.

BEN : (cutting her off) And I have to decide which cases we're gonna devote our very limited resources to.

VERONICA : I will do all of the legwork, Mr. Forsik. But since I don't have any experience in death penalty cases, I'm just asking you to point me in the right direction.

Ben and Nick both just look at her. Ben sighs.

VERONICA : (quietly pleading) Please.

BEN : I'm sorry. We just don't have the manpower.

Veronica is stunned and disappointed. She wants to say something more, but decides against it.

VERONICA : (watching Nick) Thank you for your time.

She stands, ready to leave.

42. EXT. PROJECT JUSTICE BUILDING. DAY
Veronica walks out to her car.
The camera swings to a dark car parked ahead her car.
Agent Hale watches her from the side mirror of his car and then dials a number on his cell phone.

베로니카 : 도와주세요. 무고한 사람을 죽게 해서는 안 되니까요. 그게 위원회의 로비에 쓰인 글귀이기도 하고요.

벤 : (불친절하지는 않게) 그런 요청이 수 천 건이요.

베로니카 : (재빨리) 물론 그러시겠죠.

벤 : (그녀의 말을 막으며) 자원이 제한되어 있는 만큼 선별을 해야만 하죠.

베로니카 : 실제 조사는 제가 다 하겠어요, 포식 씨. 하지만 사형 사건의 소송 경험이 없으니까 제가 바른 길을 가도록 도와달라는 것 뿐입니다.

벤과 닉 둘 다 그녀를 바라본다. 벤은 한숨을 짓는다.

베로니카 : (조용히 간청하며) 부탁해요.

벤 : 미안하오. 그럴 만한 인력이 없어요.

베로니카는 아연실색하며 실망한다. 그녀는 뭔가 더 말하고 싶지만 안 하기로 결정한다.

베로니카 : (닉을 응시하며) 시간 내주셔서 감사합니다.

그녀는 나갈 준비를 하면서 일어선다.

42. 외부. 사법 정의 위원회 건물. 낮

베로니카가 걸어나와 차로 간다.
카메라가 돌면서 그녀의 차 앞쪽에 주차되어 있는 짙은 색 차를 비춘다.
헤일 요원이 자신의 차 옆 거울을 통해 그녀를 보고는 휴대전화의 번호를 돌린다.

■ **representation**
진정, 항의, 설명, 진술
- formal statements made to somebody in authority, especially in order to make your opinions known or to protest

■ **cut off**
가로막다, 끊다
- to block or get in the way of something

■ **resources**
자원, 수단, 재원, 방책, 자산, 공급원, 기략, 소질

I will do all of the legwork.

실제 조사는 제가 다 하겠어요.

▶ legwork은 구어로 '(범죄의) 상세한 조사, 실제적인 관리, 걸어 돌아다니기'의 뜻이다.

HALE : She's just leaving now. Figure it'll take her at least half an hour to get across town in this traffic.

Veronica's car starts moving.

43. INT. VERONICA'S APARTMENT. DAY
Kellerman is sifting through documents in her apartment.

KELLERMAN : (into an earpiece) We're not going to need nearly that much time.

He pauses and leans forward to look at something. He picks up a photo. It shows Veronica and Lincoln at her graduation from law school. Next to them is Michael in a ball cap.

KELLERMAN : I've turned up quite a bit already.

44. INT. MICHAEL'S CELL. NIGHT
Haywire straightens out his toiletries on the sink.
Indistinct chatters are heard outside.

HAYWIRE : Hey, have you seen my toothpaste? It was right here.

Michael is staring out the bars of the cell.

MICHAEL : Haven't seen it.

HAYWIRE : I always put it in the same place.

MICHAEL : I'm sure it'll turn up.

Haywire stares into the mirror, which is reflecting Michael's frame.

헤 일 : 그녀가 지금 건물을 떠나고 있습니다. 교통 상황을 감안할 때 집까지 적어도 30분쯤 걸릴 겁니다.

베로니카의 차가 움직이기 시작한다.

43. 내부. 베로니카의 아파트. 낮
켈러먼이 그녀의 아파트에서 서류를 추리고 있다.

켈러먼 : (이어폰에다) 그 정도까지는 필요 없을 거야.

그는 멈추며 뭔가를 보기 위해 몸을 앞쪽으로 내민다. 그는 사진 한 장을 든다. 거기에는 법과 대학원 졸업식장에서 찍은 베로니카와 링컨의 모습이 보인다. 그들 옆에는 마이클이 야구 모자를 쓰고 서 있다.

켈러먼 : 이미 많은 걸 찾았어.

44. 내부. 마이클의 감방. 밤
헤이와이어가 세면대 위에 자신의 화장용품을 정리한다.
밖에서 분명치 않게 떠드는 소리가 들린다.

헤이와이어 : 이봐, 내 치약 봤어? 여기 있었는데.

마이클은 감방의 철창 밖을 내다보고 있다.

마이클 : 못 봤어.
헤이와이어 : 늘 같은 곳에 둔단 말이야.
마이클 : 틀림없이 나타날 거야.

헤이와이어는 거울 속을 응시한다. 거기에는 마이클의 형체가 반사되고 있다.

- **sift**
선별하다, 가려내다, 엄밀히 조사하다
- examine something very carefully in order to decide what is important or useful or to find something important

- **earpiece**
이어폰, 수신기
- earphone
- the part of a telephone or piece of electrical equipment that you hold next to or put into your ear so that you can listen

- **ball cap**
야구 모자

I've turned up quite a bit already.
이미 많은 걸 찾았어.

▶ turn up은 '발굴하다, 발견하다, 조사하다'의 뜻이다.

C.O. : (V.O.) Lights out in ten minutes.

45. INT. SUCRE'S CELL. NIGHT
Camera closes in on Sucre. Lights are out and he lays on his bunk staring up at a photo of him with Maricruz.

46. INT. MICHAEL'S CELL. NIGHT
Michael is asleep facing the wall and Haywire is slowly ripping open parts of Michael's shirt, exposing parts of his tattoo. Suddenly Michael jumps and pushes himself against the wall. His feet are facing Haywire.

HAYWIRE : The tattoos—there's a maze.

MICHAEL : (fearful, but hiding it well) Get away from me.

HAYWIRE : I need to see 'em. I just ... you gotta show 'em to me. It's pullin' me in.

He keeps coming closer to Michael.
Michael pulls his feet into a defensive pose, close to his body.

MICHAEL : I said get away from me.

HAYWIRE : (backing up) He's got a maze on his skin. (laughs) The man's got a maze on his skin.

He gets up and moves to the cell door.

HAYWIRE : Why ... why would he do that? Why ... why would he put a maze on his skin?

Michael looks down. He knows what he has to do.

교도관　　　　: (목소리) 10분 후 소등한다.

45. 내부. 수크레의 감방. 밤

카메라는 수크레를 크게 비춘다. 불이 꺼지고 그는 침대에 누워 자신과 마리 크루즈가 함께 찍은 사진을 바라보고 있다.

46. 내부. 마이클의 감방. 밤

마이클이 벽을 향해 누워 잠을 자고 있다. 헤이와이어는 천천히 마이클의 셔츠 일부를 찢어 열면서 문신의 일부를 드러내게 한다. 갑자기 마이클이 벌떡 일어나 몸을 빼내 벽에 기댄다. 그의 발이 헤이와이어를 마주하고 있다.

헤이와이어　　: 그 문신—미로가 있어.

마이클　　　　: (두려워하지만 그것을 잘 숨기면서) 저리 꺼져.

헤이와이어　　: 그걸 봐야겠어. 난… 좀 보여줘. 너무 황홀해.

그는 마이클에게 더 가까이 다가온다.
마이클은 자신의 발을 몸에 가까이 대면서 방어적인 자세를 취한다.

마이클　　　　: 저리 꺼지라고 했잖아.

헤이와이어　　: (물러서며) 피부에 미로라니. (웃는다) 피부에 미로가
　　　　　　　　새겨져 있어.

그는 일어나 감방 문으로 움직인다.

헤이와이어　　: 왜… 왜 그랬을까? 왜… 왜 피부에 미로 문신을
　　　　　　　　새겼을까?

마이클은 시선을 떨군다. 그는 자신이 무엇을 해야 할지를 알고 있다.

- **rip**

　찢다, 째다, 잡아 찢다

- to tear something or to become torn, often suddenly or violently
- to remove something quickly or violently, often by pulling it

- **expose**

　~을 드러내다, 노출시키다, 나타내다, 내놓다

- to show something that is usually hidden
- to tell the true facts about a person or a situation, and show them/it to be immoral, illegal, etc.

- **maze**

　미로, 미궁, 미로같이 복잡함

- a system of paths separated by walls or hedges built in a park or garden, that is designed so that it is difficult to find your way through

I said get away from me.

내가 꺼지라고 했잖아.

▶ I said, "Get away from me." 를 묘출화법으로 표현한 문장이다.

HAYWIRE   : Um, I don't know.

He sticks his finger into his mouth and Michael continues to watch him.
The shot moves through the tunnels of the prison.

47. EXT. FOX RIVER PENITENTIARY. DAY
The camera pans over the Fox River.

48. EXT. PRISON YARD. DAY
Abruzzi is walking on the sidewalk and Michael hurries to catch up with Abruzzi. He
looks back at Haywire.

MICHAEL   : How are your contacts in Chemical Lockup?

ABRUZZI   : Depends. Who's asking?

MICHAEL   : I need a bottle of drain line root control. Sooner than
             later.

ABRUZZI   : You got weeds growin' in your cell?

The shot goes to Haywire walking, fidgeting with his sketchbook.

MICHAEL   : (V.O.) Just one.

They walk off as Haywire glances at his sketchbook and back at Michael.

49. EXT. CHICAGO POLICE STATION. DAY
Veronica talks to Officer Weston outside the police station in Chicago.

WESTON   : You the one that's lookin' for me?

VERONICA   : Yeah, I wanted to ask you some questions about the
              Lincoln Burrows case.

헤이와이어　　：음, 모르겠어.

그는 손가락을 입에 넣는데 마이클은 계속 그를 지켜본다.
카메라는 교도소의 터널을 통해 움직여 간다.

47. 외부. 폭스 리버 교도소. 낮
카메라가 폭스 리버를 비춘다.

48. 외부. 교도소 운동장. 낮
아브루치가 인도를 걸어가고 있는데 마이클이 서둘러 아브루치를 따라붙는다.
그는 헤이와이어를 뒤돌아본다.

마이클　　：화약 약품 창고에 줄 있어?
아브루치　　：형편에 달렸지. 누가 찾는데?
마이클　　：잡초 제거제가 필요해. 가능한 한 빨리.
아브루치　　：감방 안에 잡초라도 자라나?

카메라는 헤이와이어가 자신의 스케치북을 만지작거리면서 걷고 있는 것을 비춘다.

마이클　　：(목소리) 딱 한 병.

그들은 자리를 뜨는데 헤이와이어는 스케치북과 마이클에게 시선을 던진다.

49. 외부. 시카고 경찰서. 낮
베로니카가 시카고의 경찰서 밖에서 웨스턴 경찰관에게 말을 하고 있다.

웨스턴　　：절 찾으셨어요?
베로니카　　：네, 링컨 버로스 사건에 대해 좀 물어볼 게 있어
　　　　　서요.

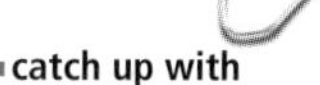

- **catch up with**
  ~를 따라붙다
  - to reach somebody who is ahead
    by going faster
  - to reach the same level or
    standard as somebody who was
    better or more advanced

- **lockup**
  〈구어〉 유치장, 교도소, 점포, 임대 창고

- **fidget**
  조바심하다, 안달하다, 만지작거리다
  - to keep moving your body, your
    hands or your feet because you
    are nervous, bored, excited, etc.

Depends.
형편에 달렸지.

▶ It〔That〕 depends.의 준 표현으로 '그것〔모두〕은 때와 장소〔형편〕에 달렸다'의 뜻임.

WESTON   : Yeah?

VERONICA   : I'm Veronica Donovan.

She shakes his hand.

VERONICA   : I'm representing Lincoln on his appeal.

WESTON   : What about it?

He starts walking toward a food vendor. She hurries to catch up with him.

VERONICA   : You were the first one to respond to Lincoln's apartment the night of the murder, right?

WESTON   : That's right.

VERONICA   : Look, I'd really appreciate it if you could just tell me exactly what you saw.

WESTON   : (stops) Dispatch called in with a tip that Burrows was seen running from the garage where they found Terrence Steadman. So we went over to Burrows' place.

Flashback.

50. INT. LINCOLN'S APARTMENT. NIGHT
Weston bursts open the door of Lincoln's apartment to find him over the sink looking slightly bewildered.

WESTON   : (V.O.) We spread out. I took the bathroom. That's where I saw your client washin' out the bloody pants.

웨스턴   : 네?
베로니카   : 베로니카 도노반입니다.

그녀는 그와 악수를 나눈다.

베로니카   : 링컨의 변호를 맡고 있어요.
웨스턴   : 그 사건에 대해 뭐가 궁금한데요?

그는 한 음식 노점상을 향해 걷기 시작한다. 그녀는 서둘러 그를 따라간다.

베로니카   : 살인 사건이 있던 날 밤 처음 링컨의 아파트에
                 가셨던데, 그렇죠?
웨스턴   : 맞아요.
베로니카   : 정확히 뭘 목격했는지 말씀해 주시면 정말 고맙
                 겠는데요.
웨스턴   : (멈춘다) 테렌스 스테드먼이 발견된 주차장에서 버로
                 스가 도망쳤다길래 버로스의 아파트로 갔죠.

플래시백.

50. 내부. 링컨의 아파트. 밤
웨스턴이 링컨의 아파트 문을 부시듯 열어젖히며 들어와 그가 약간 당황한 표
정으로 세면대에 있는 것을 발견한다.

웨스턴   : (목소리) 그래서 욕실로 갔더니 버로스가 피 묻은
                 바지를 빨고 있었어요.

- **appeal**
  〈법률〉 항소, 상고, 상소
  - a formal request to a court of law or to somebody in authority for a judgment or a decision to be changed

- **vendor**
  노점상, 행상인
  - a person who sells things, for example food or newspapers, usually outside on the street

- **dispatch**
  급송 공문서, 급파, 특파
  - a message or report sent quickly from one military officer to another or between government officials

- **bewildered**
  당황한, 어리둥절한
  - confused, embarrassed
    - bewilder
      당황하게 하다, 어리둥절하게 하다
      - to confuse something

What about it?
그것에 대해 뭐가 궁금한데요?

▶ What do you want about it?가 줄어든 표현이다.

In flashback the police officer points a gun at the defenseless Lincoln.

WESTON   : Police! Hands up!

End flashback.

51. EXT. CHICAGO POLICE STATION. DAY

WESTON   : I don't need to tell you it was Steadman's blood, do I?

VERONICA   : In the report that you typed up that night, you said that you saw Lincoln standing in the bathroom. That's all.

Weston nods.

VERONICA   : Later, you testified that you saw him washing the pants. Which one is it?

WESTON   : Does it matter?

VERONICA   : Did you actually see him washing the pants or not?

WESTON   : Yes. He stood up, turned around, his hands were all wet, looking guilty as hell.

VERONICA   : Your testimony factored into his conviction. You know that, right?

WESTON   : (laughing in disbelief) Oh, you know, lady, if you got any other questions, just go through the department.

He walks off. Veronica watches him leave, thinking about the conversation. She walks to her car and begins to unlock the door when Nick Savrinn appears beside her.

플래시백에서 경찰관은 방어를 하지 않는 링컨에게 총을 겨눈다.

웨스턴　　　：경찰이다! 손 들어!

플래시백이 끝난다.

51. 외부. 시카고 경찰서. 낮

웨스턴　　　：스테드먼의 피란 건 굳이 말할 필요 없겠죠?
베로니카　　：당신이 그날 밤 작성한 보고서에는 링컨이 욕실
　　　　　　에 서 있었다고만 적었는데.

웨스턴은 고개를 끄덕인다.

베로니카　　：나중에 당신은 그가 바지를 빨고 있었다고 진술
　　　　　　했는데 뭐가 진실이죠?
웨스턴　　　：그게 문제가 되나요?
베로니카　　：그가 바지 빠는 걸 정말 보셨어요, 아니에요?
웨스턴　　　：네. 그가 일어서서 돌아섰을 때 손이 모두 젖어
　　　　　　있었고 죄지은 표정이었소.
베로니카　　：당신 증언이 유죄 판결의 결정적 역할 한 거 알
　　　　　　아요?
웨스턴　　　：(불신의 표정으로 웃으면서) 이봐요, 아가씨, 또 궁금
　　　　　　한 게 있으면 절차를 밟아 하시오.

그는 걸어간다. 베로니카는 나눈 대화를 생각하면서 그가 가는 것을 지켜본
다. 그녀는 자신의 차로 걸어가 문을 열기 시작하는데 그때 닉 새브린이 그녀
옆에서 모습을 보인다.

- **defenseless**
  무방비 상태의, 방어할 수 없는

- **as hell**
  〈구어〉 매우 지독하게
  - used for emphasis

- **testimony**
  (법정에서의) (선서) 증언, 공술서, 고백
  - a formal written or spoken statement saying what you know to be true, usually in a court of law

- **factor**
  하나의 요인으로 포함하다, 계산에 넣다
  - to include a particular fact or situation when you are thinking about or planning something

- **conviction**
  〈법률〉 유죄의 판결
  - the act of finding somebody guilty of a crime in a court of law; the fact of having been found guilty

Does it matter?

그게 문제가 되나요?

▶ matter는 주로 의문문, 부정문, 조건문에서 '문제가 되다, 중요하다'의 뜻이 된다.

NICK   : Ms. Donovan.

She jumps slightly and looks up. Nick puts his hands up defensively.

NICK   : I ... I didn't mean to scare you.

VERONICA   : What are you doin' here?

NICK   : Nick Savrinn with Project Justice.

VERONICA   : (impatient) I know who you are, but what are you doin' here?

NICK   : (getting closer) Look, my boss may not think Lincoln's case is worth looking into, but I do.

52. EXT. PRISON YARD. DAY
There is a shot of Haywire standing by a fence furiously sketching in his sketchpad. The camera pulls forward to reveal him looking across at Michael. Michael, his back to him, sighs and turns to look at Abruzzi as he approaches and sits down, a bottle in his hand.

ABRUZZI   : There's a quicker way to take care of your problem.

He slides the bottle of drain line out of his hand to expose the shank. Michael raises an eyebrow and pauses.

MICHAEL   : There's smarter ways, too.

He takes the bottle from Abruzzi, leaving the shank. He walks off. Abruzzi watches him leave and tucks the shank down his sleeve.

닉   : 미즈 도노반.

그녀는 약간 물러나 쳐다본다. 닉은 방어적으로 손을 든다.

닉   : 당신을 놀래 주려던 건 아니었어요.

베로니카   : 여긴 웬일이세요?

닉   : 사법 정의 위원회의 닉 새브린입니다.

베로니카   : (초조해서) 누군진 알아요, 근데 여긴 웬일이냐고
                요?

닉   : (더 가까이 다가서며) 제 상관과 달리 전 링컨의 사건
                을 재조사해야 한다고 생각하거든요.

52. 외부. 교도소 운동장. 낮

카메라는 스케치북에다가 열심히 스케치를 하면서 울타리 옆에 서 있는 헤이
와이어를 비춘다. 카메라가 다시 다가가 그가 마이클을 건너다보고 있는 것을
비춘다. 마이클은 그에게 등을 돌린 채 한숨을 쉬며 돌아서서 아브루치를 바
라보는데 그가 손에 병을 들고 다가와 앉는다.

아브루치   : 골칫덩이를 제거하는 데는 더 빠른 방법도 있어.

그는 자신의 손에서 잡초 제거제 병을 밀어내며 손잡이 칼을 나타내 보인다.
마이클은 눈썹을 치켜 뜨며 잠시 시간을 둔다.

마이클   : 좀 더 현명한 방법도 있지.

그는 아브루치로부터 그 병을 받아 들지만 칼은 남겨둔다. 그는 사라진다.
아브루치는 그가 가는 것을 바라보다가 그 칼을 소매 아래로 밀어 넣는다.

■ tuck

~을 밀어 넣다, 쑤셔 넣다, 걷어 올리
다, 감싸다
- to push, fold or turn the euds or
  edges of clothes, paper, etc. so
  that they are held in place or look
  neat

I didn't mean to scare you.

당신을 놀라게 할 의도는 아니었어요.

▶ mean to는 '~할 작정이다, ~하려고 의도하다'의 뜻이다.

53. INT. MICHAEL'S CELL. NIGHT
He uncoils an empty toothpaste tube. The shot shows the bottles of drain line root control and masonry cleaner.

C.O. : (V.O.) Ten minutes. Lights out in ten minutes.

Flashback.

54. INT. MICHAEL'S APARTMENT. DAY
Scribbled over an equation are the words "Cute Poison" in red. In the flashback, Michael does a lab test. He slips a drop of liquid from a pipette onto metal.
End flashback.
Michael pours the masonry cleaner into a tube of toothpaste.
Flashback.
Michael drops a drop of a black liquid that looks very similar to the masonry cleaner onto the liquid already on the metal. Together they bubble in a chemical reaction.
End flashback.

55. INT. MICHAEL'S CELL. NIGHT
Michael screws on the lids of two tubes of toothpaste and holds them up together.

56. EXT. CHICAGO. RESTAURANT. DAY
Nick and Veronica meet in a cafe. They are having coffee.

NICK : What stood out for me was that most death penalty cases take ten years to exhaust all appeals. Lincoln got there in three.

VERONICA : So for it to be expedited, there had to have been some sort of political influence, right?

NICK : Well, given that Terrence Steadman is the Vice President's brother, that's not too hard to believe.

53. 내부. 마이클의 감방. 밤

그는 빈 치약 튜브를 다시 편다. 카메라는 석조용 잡초 제거제 병을 비춘다.

교도관 : (목소리) 10분이다. 10분 후 소등한다.

플래시백.

54. 내부. 마이클의 아파트. 낮

방정식 위에 빨간 글씨로 '짜릿한 독극물'이란 단어가 갈겨 쓰여 있다. 플래시백에서 마이클은 실험실 테스트를 한다. 그는 금속 위에다 피펫관으로부터 액체를 떨어뜨린다.
플래시백이 끝난다.
마이클은 석조용 잡초 제거제를 치약 튜브에 붓는다.
플래시백.
마이클은 이미 금속 위에 있는 액체 위에다 석조용 잡초 제거제와 아주 유사한 검은 액체를 떨어뜨린다. 그것들은 함께 화학 반응을 일으키며 부글부글 거품을 낸다.
플래시백이 끝난다.

55. 내부. 마이클의 감방. 밤

마이클은 두 개의 치약 튜브 뚜껑을 돌려 닫고는 그것들을 함께 들어본다.

56. 외부. 시카고.레스트랑. 낮

닉과 베로니카가 카페에서 만난다. 그들은 커피를 마시고 있다.

닉 : 대개 사형 판결은 항소심을 끝내는 데 10년이 걸리는데 링컨의 경우 3년이 걸렸다는 게 특이했어요.

베로니카 : 그러니까 그 사건은 정치적 영향력이 작용해 재빨리 처리됐단 건가요?

닉 : 테렌스 스테드먼은 부통령의 동생이니 믿기 힘든 것도 아니죠.

- **scribble**
  갈겨 쓰다, 낙서하다, 날려 쓰다
  - to write something quickly and carelessly, especially because you do not have much time
  - to draw marks that do not mean anything

- **pipette**
  피펫(극소량의 액체 등을 재거나 옮기는 데 쓰는 작은 관)
  - a narrow tube used in a laboratory for measuring or transferring small amounts of liquids

so for it to be expedited
그러니까 그걸 재빨리 저리히려고

▶ expedite은 '~을 재빨리 처리하다' for it은 to be expedited의 의미상 주어임.

VERONICA   : How, though? They got to every judge that rejected Lincoln's appeal?

NICK   : (shaking his head) It doesn't take a judge.

He takes a sip of water.

NICK   : All it takes is a little special attention from one of his clerks. But how Lincoln got fast-tracked doesn't interest me. It's why. If he was set up, then why?

VERONICA   : I think the answer to that might lie in the victim. What do we know? That he was the CEO of Ecofield, right?

Nick nods.

VERONICA   : That he was pushing alternative energy.

Nick interrupts and holds up a finger.

NICK   : Successfully pushing alternative energy. So oil companies, the Saudis, even... even our own government—a lot of people stood to benefit with Steadman out of the picture

Veronica drinks from her coffee cup.

NICK   : Why did you wait till now to take up his case?

베로니카   : 어떻게요? 링컨의 항소를 거절한 판사들을 강요 해서요?

닉   : (고개를 흔들면서) 판사를 끌어들일 것도 없죠.

그는 물 한 모금을 마신다.

닉   : 법원 서기관에게 압력만 넣으면 되니까요. 그보 다 왜 하필 링컨을 함정에 빠뜨렸는가가 중요해 요. 그가 함정에 빠졌다면 왜일까요?

베로니카   : 그 해답은 희생자가 쥐고 있겠죠. 우리가 뭘 알 겠어요? 그가 에코필드사 사장이었다면서요?

닉이 고개를 끄덕인다.

베로니카   : 그가 대체 에너지 사업을 추진 중이었다는데.

닉이 말을 막으며 손가락을 쳐든다.

닉   : 대체 에너지를 성공적으로 밀어붙였죠. 그래서 그가 없어지면 정유 회사나 사우디, 심지어… 우 리 정부까지, 많은 사람들이 이득을 보죠.

베로니카는 커피 잔에서 커피를 마신다.

닉   : 왜 여태 있다가 그의 사건을 맡은 거죠?

■ **fast-tracked**
서둘러 처리된
- fast-track
  서둘러 처리하다

■ **CEO**
최고 경영자(chief executive officer (the person with the highest rank in a business company)의 약어)

■ **alternative**
대신의, 양자택일의, 기존의 방식과는 전혀 다른
- that can be used instead of something else
- different from the usual or traditional way in which something is done

■ **out of the picture**
동떨어진, 얼토당토않은, 상황에 포함 되지 않은
- not involved in a situation

It doesn't take a judge.
그건 판사가 필요없어요.

▶ take는 it를 주어로 "~이 필요하다, ~이 들다, ~걸린다"의 뜻이다.

VERONICA : I thought he did it, like everybody else. I just hope it's not too late.

NICK : (nodding) It very well may be. (leans back in his chair) You need to prepare yourself for that.

She doesn't want to believe that.

VERONICA : What about you?

Nick looks up.

VERONICA : Why death penalty work?

NICK : My father did fifteen years for a crime he didn't commit. I know firsthand that when the government gets you in their cross-hairs, you stand very little chance. That's why.

Veronica looks concerned. Nick leans forward.

NICK : Now, do you want my help?

57. EXT. PRISON YARD. DAY
Michael walks into the yard, as Haywire watches him enter. As he walks past him, Haywire is drawing a pattern on his notepad. He freezes in realization.
Sucre strides across the yard to Michael, a purposeful and worried look on his face.

SUCRE : I want back in.

MICHAEL : Too late.

| 베로니카 | : 다른 사람들처럼 링컨이 유죄라고 생각했거든요. 너무 늦지 않았기를 바랄 뿐이에요. |
| 닉 | : (고개를 끄덕이며) 그럴 가능성이 많죠. (의자에 기댄다) 각오는 해두도록 해요. |

그녀는 그것을 믿고 싶지 않다.

| 베로니카 | : 당신은요? |

닉이 쳐다본다.

| 베로니카 | : 왜 사형 사건에 관심을 가진 거죠? |
| 닉 | : 아버지가 누명을 쓰고 15년간 복역하셨거든요. 정부의 표적이 되면 옴짝달싹 못한다는 걸 알아요. 그게 이유죠. |

베로니카는 근심어린 표정이다. 닉이 몸을 앞으로 내민다.

| 닉 | : 자, 제 도움이 필요한가요? |

57. 외부. 교도소 운동장. 낮

마이클이 운동장으로 들어오는데 헤이와이어는 그가 들어오는 것을 지켜본다. 마이클이 자신의 옆으로 지나가자 헤이와이어는 메모장에다가 한 형태를 그리고 있다. 그는 뭔가 알아채고는 그 자리에 꼼짝 않고 선다.
수크레가 운동장을 가로질러 마이클을 향해 성큼 다가온다. 얼굴에는 뭔가 결단을 내린 듯하고 근심이 어려 있는 표정이다.

| 수크레 | : 나도 낄래. |
| 마이클 | : 너무 늦었어. |

■ **firsthand**
직접(으로), 바로, 직접 체험으로
- at first hand

■ **cross-hairs**
(망원경 등의 초점에 새긴) 십자선
- reticle
- a shape superimposed on an image that is used for precise alignment of a device
- Crosshairs are most commonly a "+" shape, though many variations exist, including dots, posts, circles, and chevrons.

■ **notepad**
메모장, 메모지 철
- sheets of paper that are held together at the top and used for writing notes on

■ **purposeful**
의도적인, 과단성 있는, 결단을 내린
- having a useful purpose; acting with a clear aim and with determination

It very well may be.
그럴 가능성이 많죠.

▶ It may be late.를 very well이 강조하는 표현이다.

SUCRE : (desperate) I'll do anything you need. See these hands? They're digging machines. You wanna go to China? I'll get you to China, fish. I'll dig like a psychotic rodent if I have to.

He crosses in front of Michael and physically blocks his path.

SUCRE : Fish, I gotta be back in.

MICHAEL : As of right now, there is no in.

He turns to look at Haywire so that Sucre follows his eye line.
Haywire is still frantically drawing.

MICHAEL : Van Gogh over there's my new cellmate.

Sucre barely gives him a glance.

SUCRE : But you're gonna do something about it, right? You gotta get rid of him.

MICHAEL : (evenly) I'll do what's necessary.

Sucre smiles and laughs, tightly hugging Michael.

SUCRE : You're my boy.

Michael smiles too.

수크레   : (필사적으로) 네가 원하는 건 뭐든지 하겠어. 이 손 보이지? 구멍 파는 기계야. 원한다면 중국까지도 팔 수 있어, 신참. 그래야 한다면 미친 쥐처럼 팔게.

그는 마이클 앞쪽으로 돌아서며 몸으로 그가 가는 길을 막는다.

수크레   : 신참, 들어가게 해줘.
마이클   : 지금 현재는 들어올 수 없어.

그가 돌아서 헤이와이어를 바라보자 수크레의 눈이 그의 시선을 따라간다. 헤이와이어는 여전히 미친 듯이 그리고 있다.

마이클   : 저기 반 고흐 선생이 새 빵 동기거든.

수크레는 그에게 거의 시선을 주지 않는다.

수크레   : 하지만 가만 있지 않을 거잖아? 그를 제거할 거잖아.
마이클   : (차분하게) 필요하다면.

수크레는 미소를 짓고는 마이클을 힘차게 포옹하면서 웃는다.

수크레   : 넌 내 구세주야.

마이클도 미소를 짓는다.

■ **psychotic**
정신병의, 정신병을 앓는
 - of or suffering from psychosis

■ **rodent**
(쥐 · 다람쥐 등의) 설치류의 동물
 - any small animal that belongs to a group of animals with strong sharp front teeth. Mice, rats and rabbits are all rodents.

■ **get rid of**
~을 제거하다, 죽이다, ~을 그만두다, ~을 벗어나다
 - to make yourself free of somebody /something that is annoying you or that you do not want
 - to throw something away

As of right now, there is no in.
지금 현재는 들어올 수 없어.

▶ as of는 '(지금) 현재의'의 뜻이고, in은 구어로 '입장할 방법'의 뜻이다.

SUCRE : So how you gonna do it?

MICHAEL : Well, let's just put it this way. Someone's gonna get hurt.

Sucre nods. He looks over at Haywire, who is still drawing.

수크레	: 그래, 어떻게 할 건데?
마이클	: 이것만은 알려주지. 누군가 다치게 될 거란 거.

수크레는 고개를 끄덕인다. 그는 아직도 그림을 그리고 있는 헤이와이어를 건너다본다.

■ **put**
표현하다, 진술하다, 말하다
- to express or state something in a
  particular way

4

스코필드는 내일 다른 교도소로 이감돼

SCOFIELD IS GETTING SHIPPED OUT TOMORROW

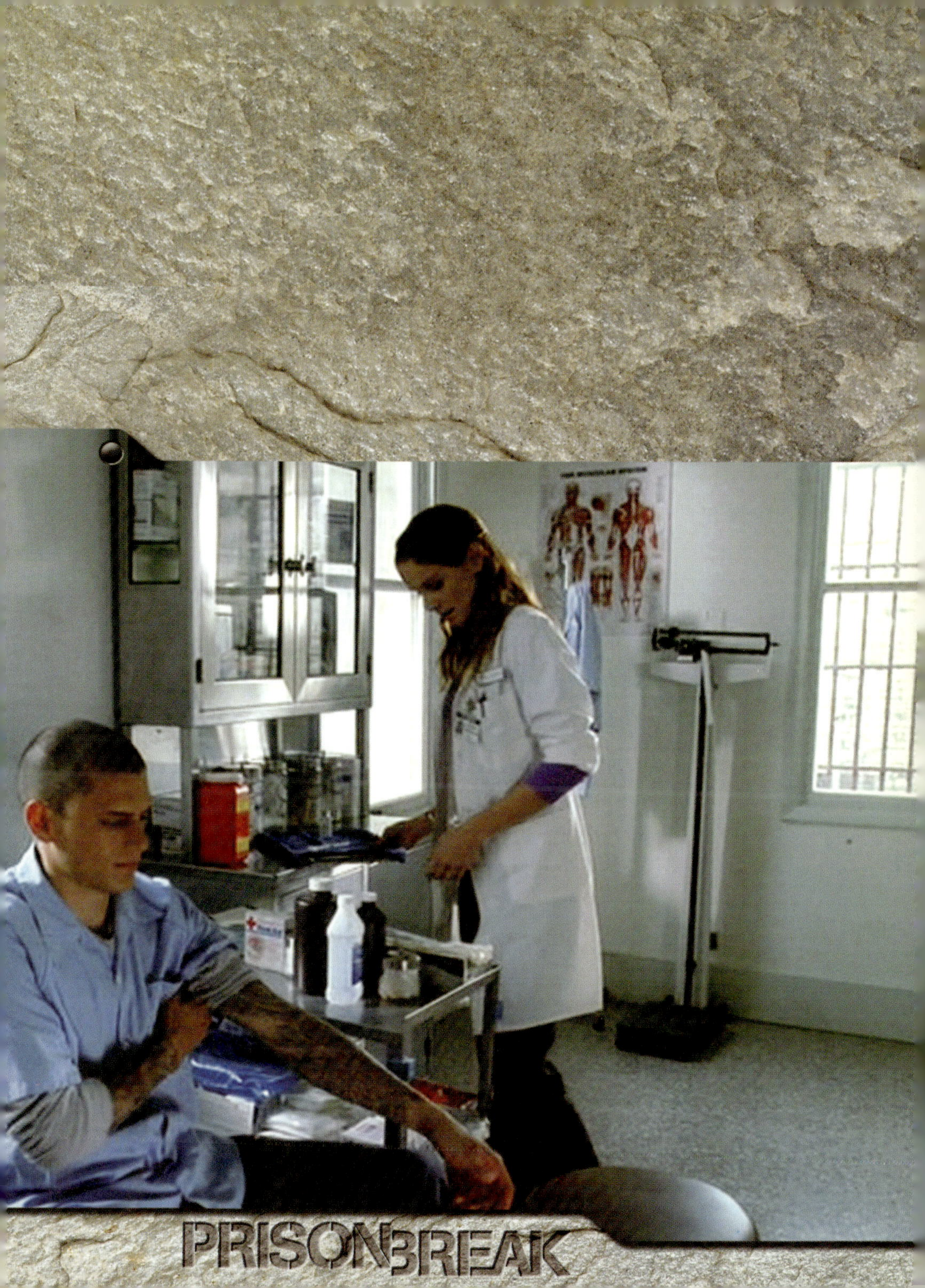

PRISONBREAK

58. EXT. COUNTRYSIDE. DAY

59. INT. GARLIC CUTTER'S HOUSE. DAY
A phone rings at the lake house in Montana. The Garlic Cutter picks up a large cutting knife and answers it slicing through a red bell pepper.

GARLIC CUTTER : How'd we miss this, guys?

60. INT. KELLERMAN'S CAR. DAY
Kellerman is driving his car through a street. Hale sits beside him.

KELLERMAN : Scofield's father was out of the picture by the time he was born. He took his mother's maiden name.

61. INT. GARLIC CUTTER'S HOUSE. DAY

GARLIC CUTTER : (still chopping) All right, Scofield had no priors and a full-time job as an engineer.

KELLERMAN : (V.O.) Correct.

GARLIC CUTTER : Then he goes and robs a bank, discharging a gun in the process, so that at sentencing he could maneuver his way to Fox River ...

62. INT. KELLERMAN'S CAR. DAY

GARLIC CUTTER : (V.O.) ... where his brother's scheduled to die in less than a month. Obviously, something's up.

58. 외부. 시골. 낮

59. 내부. 마늘 써는 사람의 집. 낮
몬태나의 호숫가 집에서 전화가 울린다. 마늘 써는 사람이 큰 칼을 집어들고
빨간 양고추를 자르면서 전화를 받는다.

마늘 써는 사람 : 어떻게 그런 걸 몰랐나?

60. 내부. 켈러먼의 차. 낮
켈러먼이 차를 몰고 거리를 지나가고 있다. 헤일이 옆에 앉아 있다.

켈러먼 : 스코필드가 태어날 때쯤 아버지가 사라지게 되자
어머니의 처녀 때 성을 받은 겁니다.

61. 내부. 마늘 써는 사람의 집. 낮

마늘 써는 사람 : (여전히 마늘을 썰며) 좋아, 스코필드는 전과도 없고
엔지니어란 직업도 있었다고?
켈러먼 : (목소리) 그렇습니다.
마늘 써는 사람 : 그러다 은행을 털고 범행 중 총까지 쏴서 폭스
리버 교도소로 들어갔다는 건데…

62. 내부. 켈러먼의 차. 낮

마늘 써는 사람 : (목소리) … 즉 형이 한 달 있으면 사형당할 곳으로
들어갔다는 말인데. 분명히 꿍꿍이가 있어.

■ **bell pepper**
양고추, 피망
- green pepper a hollow green fruit
  that is eaten, raw or cooked, as a
  vegetable

■ **discharge**
총포를 발사하다
- to fire a gun, etc.

■ **maneuver**
계략을 써서 ~하게 하다, 조종하다
- to control or influence a situation in
  a skilful but sometimes dishonest
  way

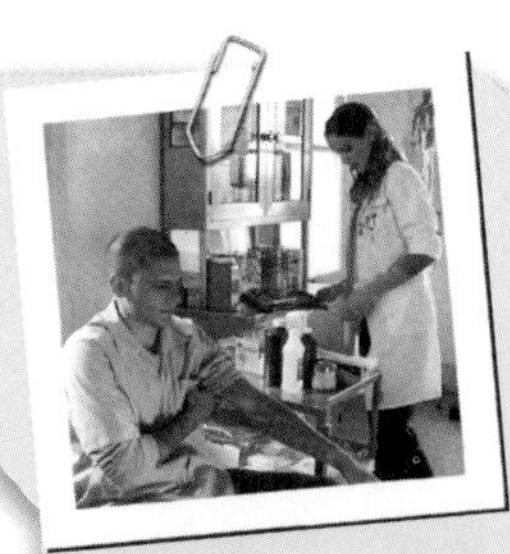

Obviously, something's up.
분명히 꿍꿍이가 있어.

▶ up은 구어로 '(일이) 생겨, 일어나'의 뜻임. Is anything up? 무슨 일인가?

HALE : All due respect, brothers are incarcerated together all over the country. It may just be a coincidence.

63. INT. GARLIC CUTTER'S HOUSE. DAY

GARLIC CUTTER : (stopping her cutting) Move on the younger brother. Do it preemptively, before anything rises up, bites any of us in the ass.

She walks off and hangs up.

64. INT. CELL BLOCK. DAY
Michael makes his way back to his cell among the inmates.

C.O. : All right, let's move it along! Let's move the line!

65. INT. MICHAEL'S CELL. CONTINUOUS
Michael walks in. Haywire has strewn out many pictures of Michael's tattoo on Michael's bunk. The cell door slides shut behind Michael.
Haywire stands up to face Michael.

HAYWIRE : It's a pathway. Where does it lead?

Michael reaches out for a sketch Haywire's holding but Haywire pulls it away.
Haywire lunges for Michael.

HAYWIRE : Where are you taking me?!

혜 일 : 외람된 말씀인데요, 형제가 같이 수용된 건 흔한 일입니다. 우연일 가능성도 있습니다.

63. 내부. 마늘 써는 사람의 집. 낮

마늘 써는 사람 : (자르기를 중단하며) 동생 녀석을 이감시켜. 우리 일에 방해되기 전에 미리 처리하란 말이야.

그녀는 걸어가며 전화를 끊는다.

64. 내부. 감방 블록. 낮
마이클이 수감자 사이에 끼어 자신의 감방으로 향한다.

교도관 : 좋아, 움직여 가자고! 줄을 움직여!

65. 내부. 마이클의 감방. 계속
마이클이 걸어 들어온다. 헤이와이어는 마이클의 침대 위에다 많은 마이클 문신 그림을 뿌려 놓았다. 마이클이 들어온 뒤 감방 문이 닫힌다. 헤이와이어는 일어서서 마이클과 얼굴을 마주한다.

헤이와이어 : 통로를 그린 거였어. 어디로 가는 통로야?

마이클은 손을 뻗쳐 헤이와이어가 펼쳐 놓은 스케치를 잡으려 하나 헤이와이어는 그것을 당긴다. 헤이와이어는 마이클에게 돌진한다.

헤이와이어 : 나를 어디로 데리고 가는 거냐고?!

- **incarcerate**
  ~을 투옥하다, 감금하다
  - to put somebody in prison or in another place from which they cannot escape

- **preemptively**
  우선적으로, 우선권이 있게

- **lunge**
  돌진하다, 갑자기 튀어 나오다
  - to make a sudden powerful forward movement in order to attack somebody

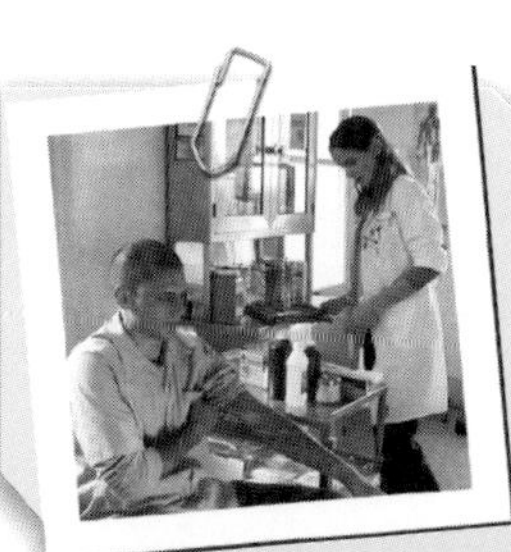

all due respect
외람된 말씀인데요

▶ 관용적인 표현으로 상대방의 말과 의견이 다를 때 점잖게 시작하는 표현이다.

Michael pushes him off, turns around and grips the bars of the cell door with his hands and slams his forehead into them twice. Haywire frowns.

HAYWIRE : What are you, nuts?

MICHAEL : (gripping his bleeding forehead) Officer! I need an officer!

INMATE : (V.O.) Shut up!

66. INT. CELL BLOCK. DAY
C.O. Patterson walks down to the cell.

C.O. PATTERSON : What the hell's the problem down here?

He turns to see the blood on Michael's fore head.

C.O. PATTERSON : What ...? Son of a bitch. Open up on forty!

The cell door slides open. Haywire points at Michael.

HAYWIRE : (pointing at Michael) He's got the pathway on his body. It leads somewhere.

C.O. PATTERSON : (finger outstretched warningly) Back off, Haywire.

Michael holds his forehead.

HAYWIRE : No, look. Look at his tattoos. It's a pathway.

C.O. PATTERSON : Haywire, I said back off. You want a hot shot?

HAYWIRE : (lunging at Michael) I'm tellin' you, look at—

마이클은 그를 밀쳐 내고 돌아서서 감방 문의 철창을 손으로 움켜쥐고는 두번에 걸쳐 이마를 창틀에 부딪친다. 헤이와이어는 이맛살을 찌푸린다.

헤이와이어 : 왜 그래, 미쳤어?

마이클 : (피가 흐르는 이마를 쥐면서) 교도관님! 와 보세요!

수감자 : (목소리) 닥쳐!

66. 내부. 감방 블록. 낮
패터슨 교도관이 감방을 걸어 내려온다.

패터슨 교도관 : 여기 도대체 무슨 일이야?

그는 돌아서서 마이클 이마의 피를 본다.

패터슨 교도관 : 왜…? 이런 망할. 40호 문 열어!

감방 문이 열린다. 헤이와이어는 마이클을 가리킨다.

헤이와이어 : (마이클을 가리키며) 몸에 통로를 새겨놨어. 어디론가 통한다고.

패터슨 교도관 : (경고하듯이 손가락을 뻗치면서) 물러서, 헤이와이어.

마이클은 자신의 이마를 잡고 있다.

헤이와이어 : 아니, 봐요. 그의 문신을 보라고요. 통로라니까.

패터슨 교도관 : 헤이와이어, 물러서라고 했다. 뜨거운 맛 좀 볼래?

헤이와이어 : (마이클에게 달려들며) 정말이라니까, 봐요—

■ **grip**
~을 꽉 잡다, 움켜 쥐다
- to hold something tightly

■ **nuts**
〈구어〉 (경멸 · 혐오 · 실망 등을 나타내어) 제기랄, 시시해, 어이없군, 바보 같은 소리; 미친, 바보의
- used to express contempt, disappointment, or refusal
- crazy
- insane

■ **outstretch**
펴다, 뻗다, 확장하다
- to stretch out
- to extend

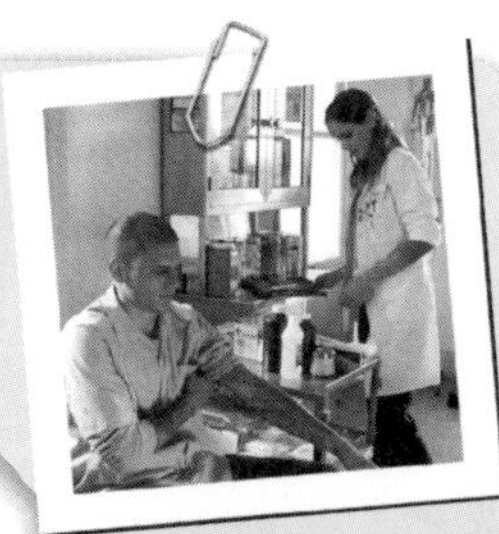

I'm tellin' you.
정말이오.

▶ 구어체의 표현으로 앞의 말을 강조하여 '정말이오', 뒤의 말을 강조하여 '내 말 잘 들어 보시오'의 뜻임.

The C.O. sprays Haywire's face with pepper spray.

HAYWIRE   : Aaaggh!

C.O. PATTERSON   : Back off!

The C.O.s apprehend him and drag him out of the cell.

C.O. PATTERSON   : Let's go! Get him outta here!

HAYWIRE   : It leads to hell! It's a pathway to hell! He's taking us all to hell!

67. INT. CELL BLOCK. DAY

C.O. Patterson exits too and Michael steps out of his cell. He watches them leave, blood dripping down his face from his forehead. The camera enters his eye and then goes through the tunnels of the prison.

68. INT. MICHAEL'S CELL. DAY

Later, Michael is sitting alone on his bunk reading a book. The cell door buzzes open and he stands up as Sucre stands outside the cell.

BELLICK   : (walking in past Sucre) So, the gang's all back together again. Well, ain't that swell?

He gets closer to Michael and lowers his voice speaking threateningly to him.

BELLICK   : Told you not to go around me to the Pope. But you just keep making waves, don't you?

교도관은 헤이와이어의 얼굴에 후추 스프레이를 뿌린다.

헤이와이어　　:아아아!
패터슨 교도관　:물러 서!

교도관들은 그를 붙잡고 감방 밖으로 끌고 간다.

패터슨 교도관　:가자고! 놈을 어서 끌어내!
헤이와이어　　:지옥으로 통한다고! 지옥으로 가는 통로라고! 저
　　　　　　　놈이 우리 모두를 지옥으로 끌고 갈 거야!

67. 내부. 감방 블록. 낮

패터슨 교도관도 나가자 마이클은 감방 밖으로 나선다. 그는 그들이 가는 것을 지켜보는데 피가 이마에서 얼굴로 흘러내리고 있다. 카메라는 그의 눈을 비추며 들어가서는 교도소의 터널을 통해 달려간다.

68. 내부. 마이클의 감방. 낮

그 후, 마이클은 책을 읽으면서 침대에 홀로 앉아 있다. 감방 문이 버저 소리와 함께 열리고 그는 수크레가 감방 밖에 서 있을 때 일어선다.

벨 릭　　:(수크레를 지나 걸어 들어오면서) 또 다시 뭉치게 됐군.
　　　　　신나겠어?

그는 마이클에게 더 가까이 다가서며 그를 위협하듯이 목소리를 낮추어 말을 한다.

벨 릭　　:소장한테 쓸데없는 소릴 말랬더니 넌 계속 말썽
　　　　　을 일으키는군.

■ **apprehend**
〈문어〉 (범인을) 체포하다
- (of the police) to catch somebody and arrest them
- to understand or recognize something

■ **swell**
〈구어〉 멋진, 훌륭한, 굉장한, 대단한
- very good, enjoyable, etc.

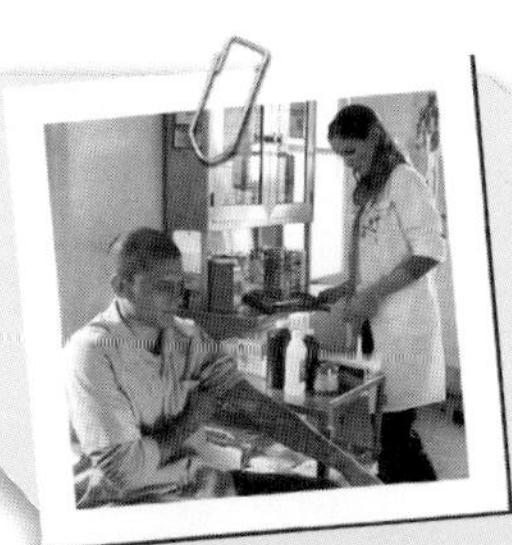

You just keep making waves, don't you?

넌 계속 밀씽을 일으키고 있어.

▶ make waves는 구어로 '풍파를 일으키다'는 뜻.

He leaves the cell and Sucre walks in, grinning. Another C.O. shuts the door and locks it.

SUCRE   : Good to be back, man.

MICHAEL   : Good to have you back.

He reaches out to shake hands while Sucre balls his fist and goes to place it on Michael's. Clumsily their hands meet. Michael balls his and Sucre clasps it in both hands and they grip each other's, slapping each other on the back.

SUCRE   : So, when do we get started?

Michael smiles.

69. INT. INFIRMARY. DAY
Dr. Tancredi can be seen through the window of the door chatting to Nurse Katie. The shot pulls back to show Michael watching. He then goes over to the grate in the corner of the room, and squeezes out the two toothpaste tubes into a drain. The liquids mix and bubble on the pipe below the sink. A hissing noise can be heard as the chemicals react together. Michael hurries back to his chair as Dr. Tancredi walks in the room.

DR. TANCREDI   : Good afternoon, Mr. Scofield.

MICHAEL   : Hello.

DR. TANCREDI   : How you feeling today?

MICHAEL   : Pretty good.

He rolls up his arm sleeve.
Dr. Tancredi notices the Band-Aid over his eyebrow.

그가 감방을 떠나자 수크레가 히죽 웃으면서 들어온다. 다른 교도관이 문을 닫고 잠근다.

수크레   : 돌아오니 기뻐, 친구.

마이클   : 네가 돌아와서 반갑다.

그는 악수하기 위해 손을 뻗치는데 수크레는 주먹을 공같이 둥글게 만들어 그 것을 마이클의 주먹 위에 놓으려 한다. 서투르게 그들의 손이 마주친다. 마이 클은 자신의 주먹을 둥글게 만들자 수크레가 양손으로 그것을 꼭 쥔다. 그들 은 서로의 등을 치면서 서로의 주먹을 움켜 잡는다.

수크레   : 그럼 언제 시작할까?

마이클은 미소를 짓는다.

69. 내부. 의무실. 낮

탠크레디 의사가 창문 밖에서 간호사인 케이티와 이야기를 나누는 것이 보인 다. 카메라는 뒤로 빠지며 마이클이 지켜보는 것을 보여준다. 그리고는 마이 클이 방의 구석에 있는 하수구 쇠살대로 가서는 두 치약 튜브를 짜서 하수구 로 집어넣는다. 액체는 섞이면서 하수구 아래 파이프에서 부글거린다. 화학 물질이 서로 반응을 하면서 지글지글 하는 소리가 들린다. 마이클은 탠크레디 의사가 방에 들어오자 급히 의자로 돌아온다.

탠크레디 의사   : 안녕하세요, 스코필드 씨.

마이클   : 안녕하세요.

탠크레디 의사   : 오늘은 좀 어때요?

마이클   : 아주 좋아요.

그는 팔 소매를 걷어 올린다.
탠크레디 의사가 마이클의 눈썹 위에 붙은 반창고를 목격한다.

- **ball**
  - ~을 공같이 둥글게 만들다, 뭉치다
  - to form something or be formed into the shape of a ball

- **clumsily**
  꼴사납게, 서투르게, 어색하게
  - clumsy
    서투른, 어색한, 꼴사나운
    - (of people and animals) moving or doing things in a very awkward way

- **clasp**
  ~을 꼭 쥐다, 악수하다
  - to hold something tightly in your hand
  - to hold somebody/something tightly with your arms around them

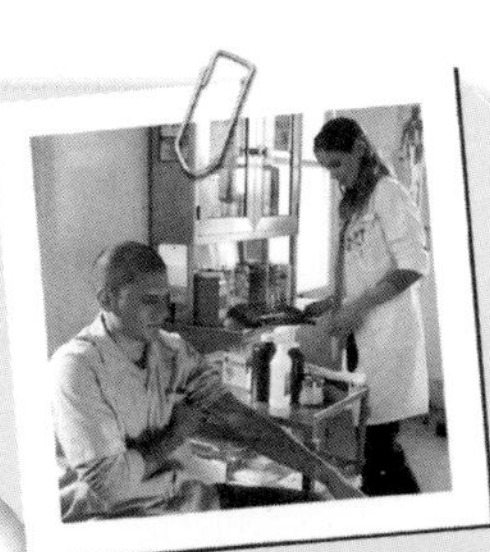

When do we get started?

언제 시작하지?

▶ get started는 '행동하기 시작하다'의 뜻이다.

DR. TANCREDI : What happened? (sits down)

MICHAEL : (shrugging) Uh, caught an elbow playing basketball.

She does not believe him.

DR. TANCREDI : Uh-huh.

She pulls on some rubber gloves.

DR. TANCREDI : Mind if I take a look?

MICHAEL : (invitingly) By all means.

Dr. Tancredi pulls off the Band-Aid and takes a look, obviously more than an elbow.

DR. TANCREDI : You know you're gonna get killed in here, right, if you're not careful?

Michael looks over at the grate.

MICHAEL : (looking at her) I'll make you a bet. When I get out of here alive, I'll take you to dinner.

She doesn't answer.

MICHAEL : Lunch. Cup of coffee.

DR. TANCREDI : Michael, this, uh, this charm act could be exactly what's getting you into trouble out in the yard.

탠크레디 의사 : 얼굴은 어쩌다가? (앉는다)
마이클 : (어깨를 으쓱하며) 아, 농구하다가 팔꿈치에 맞았어요.

그녀는 그의 말을 믿지 않는다.

탠크레디 의사 : 그래요.

그녀는 고무 장갑을 낀다.

탠크레디 의사 : 한 번 봐도 되겠어요?
마이클 : (마음이 동하듯이) 물론이죠.

탠크레디 의사는 그 반창고를 떼어내고 상처를 보는데 분명히 팔꿈치로 맞은 그 이상의 부상이다.

탠크레디 의사 : 조심하지 않으면 여기서 죽게 돼요, 알죠?

마이클은 쇠격자를 건너다본다.

마이클 : (그녀를 보면서) 내기 하나 하죠. 내가 여기서 살아서 나가면 저녁 식사에 초대하겠어요.

그녀는 대답하지 않는다.

마이클 : 점심. 커피 한 잔.
탠크레디 의사 : 마이클, 이, 어, 이 귀여운 장난 때문에 여기서 죽게 될지도 몰라요.

■ **invitingly**
유혹적으로, 마음이 동하듯이
• inviting
- making you want to do, try, taste, etc. something
- attractive

■ **by all means**
(대답을 강조하여) 좋고말고, 부디, 꼭
- used to say that you are very willing for somebody to have something or do something

■ **make a bet**
내기를 하다
• bet
내기, 걸기, 건 돈, 내기의 대상
- an arrangement to risk money, etc. on the result of a particular event
- the money that you risk in this way
- (informal) an opinion about what is likely to happen or to have happened

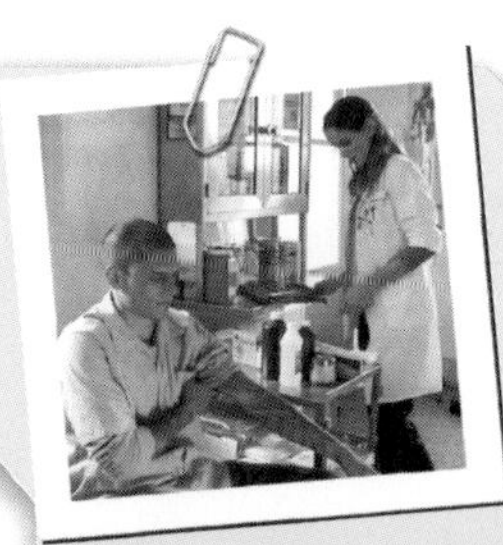

Mind if I take a look?

한 번 봐도 되겠어요?

▶ Would(Do) you mind if I take a look?과 같은 표현. 승낙의 경우, 대답은 부정으로 해야 한다.

Michael doesn't answer and looks away.

DR. TANCREDI : Lean forward.

He complies and she places a fresh bandage on his gash above his eyebrow. The shot closes in on the grate, with the mixture bubbling.

70. INT. OPEN VISITATION. DAY
Lincoln, Nick and Veronica discuss the night of the murder. Nick walks over from the window to where Lincoln and Veronica sit at the table.

NICK : All right, you went to the parking garage. Terrence Steadman is ... is already dead.

He has been pacing and stops and sits down.

LINCOLN : That's right.

NICK : You saw that, and you ran. Took the gun.

LINCOLN : (shaking his head) Dumped the gun.

NICK : Where?

LINCOLN : Storm drain. (looking at Veronica) Van Buren and Wells.

VERONICA : Nobody ever found it.

NICK : What do you do after that? You go back to your apartment?

LINCOLN : (thinking back, nodding) Yeah.

Flashback.

마이클은 대답하지 않고 시선을 돌린다.

탠크레디 의사　：앞으로 숙여요.

그는 그녀의 요구에 응하고 그녀는 그의 눈썹 위 상처에 새 붕대를 붙인다. 카메라는 쇠살대 아래에서 뒤섞여 부글거리는 장면을 비춘다.

70. 내부. 공개 면회실. 낮
링컨, 닉 그리고 베로니카가 살인 사건이 벌어진 날 밤에 대해 상의를 하고 있다. 닉이 창가로부터 링컨과 베로니카가 테이블에 앉아 있는 곳으로 다가온다.

닉　　　　：좋아요, 당신이 주차 빌딩에 갔을 땐 테렌스 스테드먼이 벌써 죽어 있었다?

그는 왔다갔다 하다가 멈춰 서서 앉는다.

링 컨　　　：맞아요.
닉　　　　：현장을 보고, 도망쳤다고요. 총을 갖고.
링 컨　　　：(고개를 가로저으며) 총은 버렸죠.
닉　　　　：어디에?
링 컨　　　：배수관에요. (베로니카를 보면서) 밴뷰렌과 웰스의 배수관요.
베로니카　：그건 아무도 못 찾았어요.
닉　　　　：그리곤 뭘 했죠? 당신 아파트로 돌아갔나요?
링 컨　　　：(회상하며 고개를 끄덕인다) 네.

플래시백.

- **comply**
  (명령, 규칙, 요구에) 응하다, 따르다, 쫓다
  - to obey a rule, an order, etc.

- **gash**
  깊은 상처, 깊이 갈라진 틈
  - a long deep cut in the surface of something, especially a person's skin

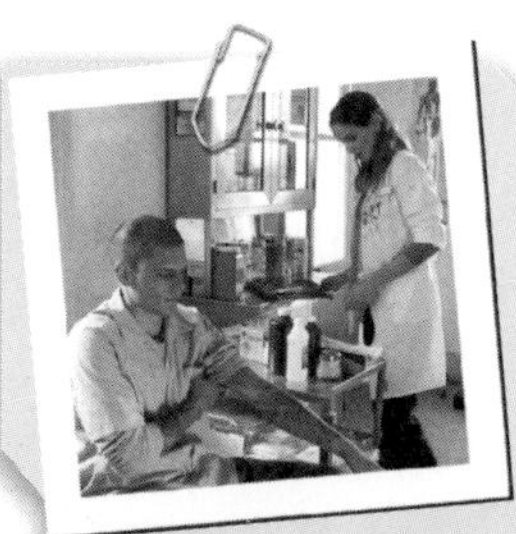

Dumped the gun.
총은 버렸다.

▶ I dumped the gun.의 준 표현으로 dump는 구어에서 '무책임하게 버리다'의 뜻으로 쓰인다.

71. INT. LINCOLN'S APARTMENT. BATHROOM. NIGHT
Lincoln washes his face in the sink.

LINCOLN : (V.O.) I was freakin' out, tryin' to figure out what had happened. Then I saw the bloody pants in the tub.

In the flashback, he walks to the bathtub.
The shot goes to the bloody pants.
End flashback.

72. INT. OPEN VISITATION. DAY
The shot goes back to Lincoln.

LINCOLN : The cops, they busted in a minute after I got there.

VERONICA : The pants, the ones with Steadman's blood on them. First cop on the scene says he saw you washing them in the bathtub.

LINCOLN : (shaking his head) He's lying. My hands were wet after splashing water on my face.

Flashback.

73. INT. LINCOLN'S APARTMENT. NIGHT
Lincoln spins around as the cops burst into his apartment.

WESTON : Police! Over your head! Hands up!

End flashback.

71. 내부. 링컨의 아파트. 욕실. 밤
링컨이 세면대에서 얼굴을 씻는다.

링 컨 : (목소리) 흥분하고 있어서 어떻게 된 건지 생각 중이었는데 그때 보니까 욕조에 피 묻은 바지가 있더군요.

플래시백에서 그는 욕조로 걸어간다.
카메라는 피 묻은 바지를 비춘다.
플래시백이 끝난다.

72. 내부. 공개 면회실. 낮
카메라는 다시 링컨에게 돌아온다.

링 컨 : 경찰은 내가 도착하고 1분도 안 돼 들이닥쳤고요.
베로니카 : 스테드먼의 피가 묻은 바지였지. 현장에 처음 도착한 경찰은 네가 그걸 욕조에서 빨고 있었다고 하던걸.
링 컨 : (고개를 저으면서) 거짓말이야. 얼굴을 씻느라고 손이 젖어 있었을 뿐이야.

플래시백.

73. 내부. 링컨의 아파트. 밤
링컨은 경찰들이 아파트에 들이 닥치자 몸을 빙 돌아선다.

웨스턴 : 경찰이다! 손 좀 봅시다! 손들어!

플래시백이 끝난다.

- **figure out**
  ~을 이해하다, 해결하다
  - to think about somebody/something until you understand them/it
  - to calculate an amount or the cost of something

- **bust**
  (경찰이) 급습하다, 현장을 덮치다, 침입하다
  - (of the police) to suddenly enter a place and search it or arrest somebody

- **on the scene**
  현장에, 그 자리에

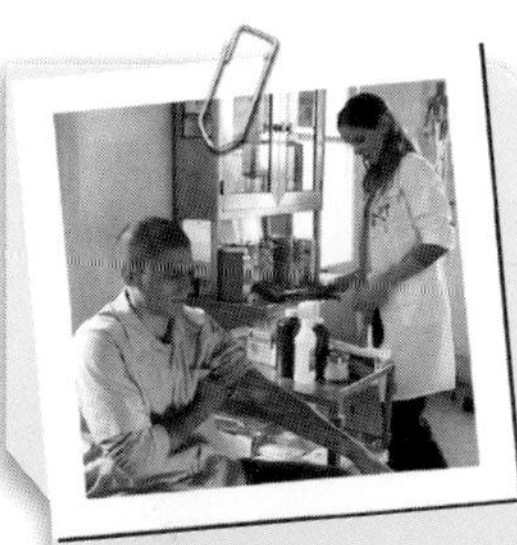

I was freakin' out.

난 흥분하고 있었다.

▶ freak out은 속어로 '(환각제로) 흥분하다, 환각 상태가 되다'의 뜻이다.

74. INT. OPEN VISITATION. DAY

LINCOLN : I never touched those pants.

NICK : (nodding) Which brings us back to the gun. The one you said you dumped.

LINCOLN : It was planted. It's the only way it could've got there.

NICK : Ballistics matched it to a slug that was—

LINCOLN : The gun was planted, it was planted. Just like the pants.

NICK : Your fingerprints were all over the gun.

Lincoln pauses in confusion. He thinks for a while and realizes.

LINCOLN : Bo.

Veronica frowns, recognition crossing her face. Nick looks confused.

NICK : Who's Bo?

LINCOLN : He's the guy who arranged everything ...

Flashback.

75. INT. PARKING GARAGE. NIGHT
Bo hands Lincoln two guns and Lincoln holds them, testing them.

74. 내부. 공개 면회실. 낮

링 컨 　：바지에는 손도 댄 적 없어.

닉 　：(고개를 끄덕이며) 그렇다면 당신이 버렸다는 총 이
　　　야기로 돌아가 보죠.

링 컨 　：누군가 일부러 갖다 놓은 게 분명해요.

닉 　：탄도 실험 결과는 총알과 일치—

링 컨 　：바지처럼 조작된 거라고요.

닉 　：총에 온통 당신 지문투성이었어요.

링컨은 혼란스러워 잠시 멈춘다. 그는 잠시 생각하더니 상황을 알아차린다.

링 컨 　：보 녀석이야.

베로니카가 이맛살을 찌푸리며 이제야 알겠다는 표정이 얼굴을 스친다. 닉은
혼란스러운 표정이다.

닉 　：보가 누구죠?

링 컨 　：이 일을 모두 계획한 놈이오…

플래시백.

75. 내부. 주차 빌딩. 밤
보는 링컨에게 총 두 자루를 건넨다. 링컨은 그것들을 받아들고 검사를 한다.

- **ballistics**
  탄도학
  - the scientific study of things that are shot or fired through the air, such as bullets and missiles

- **slug**
  (구식 총의) 납 등으로 만든 총알, (공기총의) 산탄
  - a bullet
  - a piece of metal shaped like a coin used to get things from machines, etc., sometimes illegally

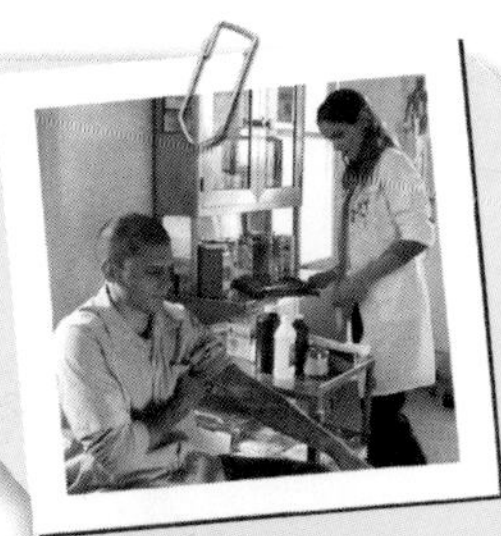

Which brings us back to the gun.
그렇다면 총 이야기로 돌아가게 된다.

▶ which는 앞의 문장을 받는 관계대명사로 이처럼 구어체에서도 흔히 쓰인다.

LINCOLN   : (V.O.) ... He had me come around the night before, try out a few guns, see which one felt right. And that was the setup right there. One of those must've been the murder weapon.

In the flashback Lincoln points to the gun he wants to use.

End flashback.

76. INT. OPEN VISITATION. DAY
The shot goes back to Lincoln.

LINCOLN   : Then that's how they got my fingerprints on the gun ... Had to be.

NICK   : All right, so this ... this ... this Bo, uh, he coerces you into doing this all to clear a ninety thousand-dollar-debt?

LINCOLN   : He was gonna kill my son.

77. EXT. FOX RIVER EXIT. DAY
Later, Nick and Veronica walk out in the parking lot of Fox River.

VERONICA   : Well?

NICK   : A lot of "I didn't do its," and those don't count for much. The security tape, the one that shows Lincoln pulling the trigger—you've got it, right?

VERONICA   : Yeah.

Nick goes around to the driver's seat of their car.

링 컨   : (목소리) 그가 사건 전날 총을 몇 자루 주면서 만져 보라고 했거든. 그때 조작된 겁니다. 그래서 살인에 쓰인 총에 내 지문이 묻었던 거죠.

플래시백에서 링컨은 자신이 사용하고 싶어하는 총을 가리킨다.

플래시백이 끝난다.

76. 내부. 공개 면회실. 낮
카메라는 다시 링컨에게 돌아온다.

링 컨   : 그렇게 해서 총에 내 지문이 묻은 겁니다. 틀림없어요.

닉   : 좋아요, 그럼 이… 이… 이 보가 9만 달러 빚을 청산하는 대신 일을 강요한 건가요?

링 컨   : 내 아들을 죽이겠다고 했었소.

77. 외부. 폭스 리버. 출구. 낮
그 후, 닉과 베로니카가 폭스 리버의 주차장으로 걸어간다.

베로니카   : 어때요?

닉   : "난 안 했다"는 말 뿐이에요. 그건 중요하지가 않아요. 링컨이 방아쇠를 당긴 장면의 테이프를 갖고 있어요?

베로니카   : 네.

닉은 차의 운전석으로 돌아간다.

- **setup**

  〈구어〉 서로 짠 경기, 고의로 계획된 일, 수월한 일
  - something done by deceit or trickery in order to compromise or frame someone

- **coerce**

  ~을 강제하다, 위압하다, 강요하다
  - to force somebody to do something by using threats

- **count for much**

  중요하다, 가치가 있다
  - to be very important

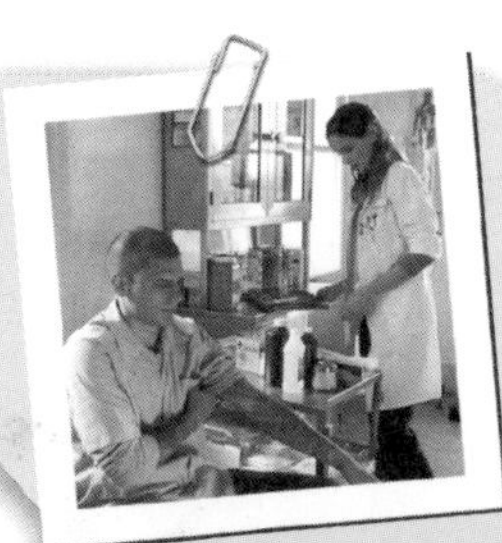

Had to be.

틀림없어요.

▶ That had to be how they got my fingerprints on the gun.의 준 표현이다.

NICK : Well, if Lincoln's telling the truth, then that tape is lying. Think we should have a look. Decide for ourselves.

They get into the car.

78. INT. MICHAEL'S CELL. NIGHT
Sucre holds out a little mirror through the bars to check for C.O.s on either side.

SUCRE : (whispering) You're clear.

Michael pulls the bolt out from under the frame of Sucre's bunk and squats down by the toilet, unscrewing the bolts in it. Sucre smiles, then picks up a tube of toothpaste discarded on Michael's bunk. He opens it and sniffs it, recoiling.

SUCRE : If the chemicals can eat through the iron pipes, how come they can't eat through a toothpaste tube?

MICHAEL : It's only when the chemicals are combined that they become a corrosive.

SUCRE : You studied chemistry or something?

MICHAEL : Not in school.

He swaps sides of the toilet to finish unscrewing it. Sucre checks outside with the mirror again and comes back to watch Michael.

SUCRE : But what you're doing up there in the infirmary, what has that gotta do with what we're doin' here?

닉   : 링컨 말이 사실이라면 그 테이프가 조작됐을 수도 있어요. 그걸 다시 보고 판단하는 게 좋겠어요.

그들은 차에 탄다.

78. 내부. 마이클의 감방. 밤
수크레가 문 창살을 통해서 작은 거울을 내밀고는 양쪽에 교도관이 있는지 조사를 한다.

수크레   : (속삭이며) 시작해.

마이클은 수크레 침대 틀 아래에서 볼트를 꺼내 변기 옆에 꾸부리고는 볼트를 넣어 나사를 돌린다. 수크레는 미소를 짓고 마이클 침대 위에 버려진 치약 튜브를 집어 든다. 그는 그것을 열고 냄새를 맡다가 움찔한다.

수크레   : 그 화학 물질이 쇠파이프를 녹인다면 왜 치약 튜브는 안전하지?
마이클   : 두 화학 물질이 합쳐져야만 부식 작용을 일으키거든.
수크레   : 화학이라도 배운 거야?
마이클   : 학교에서 배운 건 아냐.

그는 나사못 돌리기를 끝마치기 위해 변기 양쪽을 바꾼다. 수크레는 다시 거울을 들고 밖을 조사하고는 돌아와 마이클을 지켜본다.

수크레   : 한데 의무실에서 일은 이거랑 무슨 상관이야?

■ **recoil**
움찔하다, 주춤하다, 뒷걸음 치다
- to move your body quickly away from somebody/something because you find them or it frightening or unpleasant

■ **corrosive**
부식제, 부식시키는 것

■ **swap**
~을 바꾸다, 교환하다
- to give something to somebody and receive something in exchange

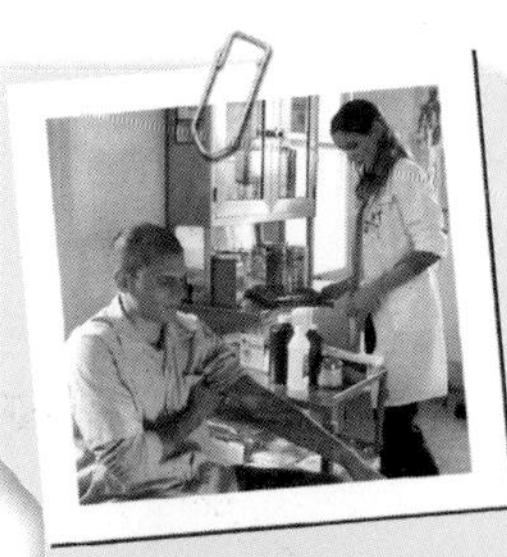

You studied chemistry or something?
화학이라도 배운 거야?

▶ or something은 구어로 '뭐라더라, ~인지 무엇인지'의 뜻이다.

MICHAEL : Getting through this wall is just the beginning. There's a whole lot of real estate in between here and the outside walls. The infirmary's the closest building to those walls.

He finally pulls the sink away from the wall.

MICHAEL : And the weakest link in the security chain.

SUCRE : (smiling) Cool.

Michael drops the bolt and picks up a piece of paper. Then he puts it through an edge in the concrete and tests the space between the bricks sink the toilet to see if they're weak enough yet.

MICHAEL : I think I've removed enough grout to bust through.

He looks back at Sucre.

MICHAEL : I'm gonna need you to make some noise.

Sucre smiles, stands up and walks over to the bars. He starts to sing in Spanish. Michael looks at him. This was not what he had in mind.

MICHAEL : (cutting him off) Is that the best you can do?

SUCRE : (smiling) Have some faith, Papi, have some faith.

He starts singing again and sure enough angry shouts begin to emerge.

마이클 　　: 이 벽을 넘어서는 건 시작에 불과해. 이 벽을 뚫
　　　　　　　고 외벽까지 가려면 거쳐야 할 게 많으니까. 의
　　　　　　　무실은 외벽과 가장 가까운 건물이거든.

그는 마침내 벽에서 세면대를 떼어낸다.

마이클 　　: 그리고 보안 사슬이 가장 약해.
수크레 　　: (미소를 지으며) 죽이네.

마이클은 볼트를 내려놓고 종이 쪽지를 집어 든다. 그리고 나서 그는 그것을
콘크리트 안의 모서리를 통해 집어넣고는 세면대 뒤쪽의 벽돌 사이에 공간이
있는지, 그것이 충분히 약한지를 본다.

마이클 　　: 뚫을 수 있을 만큼 회반죽을 제거한 것 같아.

그는 수크레를 돌아본다.

마이클 　　: 좀 시끄럽게 해줘.

수크레는 미소를 짓고는 일어서서 철창으로 걸어간다. 그는 스페인어로 노래
를 시작한다. 마이클이 그를 본다. 이건 그가 생각했던 것이 아니다.

마이클 　　: (그의 노래를 막으며) 그 정도 밖에 못 해?
수크레 　　: (웃으며) 믿어 봐, 친구, 믿어보라고.

그는 다시 노래하기 시작하는데 충분히 화가 난 외침 소리가 들리기 시작한다.

■ **real estate**
물적 재산(특히 토지), 부동산
- property in the form of land or
　buildings

■ **grout**
(쪼개진 바위 틈 등에 개어 넣는) 그라
우트, 시멘트 풀, 모르타르 풀
- a substance that is used between
　the tiles on the walls of kitchens,
　bathrooms, etc.

■ **papi**
구어체로 daddy, pop을 말한다
영어와 스페인어의 철자가 같다.

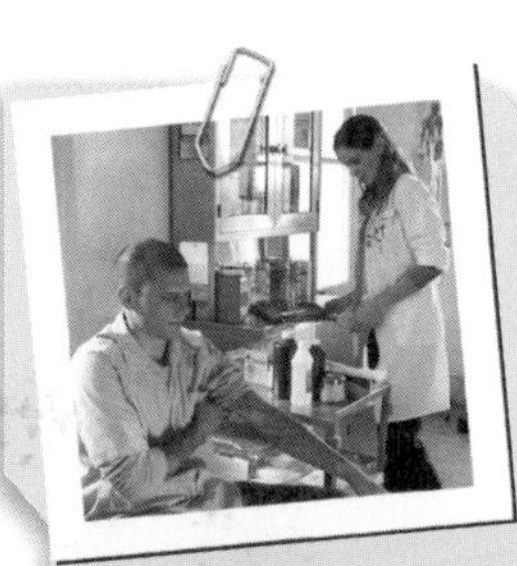

Cool.
죽인다.

▶ cool은 속어로 '멋진, 근사한'의 뜻으로 That's cool.(멋지군, 아주 좋아)가 준 표현이다.

INMATE   : (V.O.) Shut up!

Other inmates join in the yelling. Michael smiles and turns back to the concrete. He starts kicking at the wall that has been filed out with his good foot. The sounds of the inmates cover up his noise.
The buzzer sounds hard.

79. INT. LINCOLN'S CELL. NIGHT
Lincoln can hear the noise, coupled with the sounds of doors buzzing open. He jumps, his eyes opening from sleep, recalling his nightmare.

80. INT. MICHAEL'S CELL. NIGHT
Sucre's singing grows louder back in A-Wing. Michael busts through the wall. Sucre suddenly stops.

81. INT. CELL BLOCK. NIGHT
The C.O.s walk out into the floor.

BELLICK   : (shouting) Not one more word! Next inmate that opens

his mouth goes into the hole!

The C.O.s walk back off.

82. INT. MICHAEL'S CELL. NIGHT
Michael and Sucre look terrified that they'll be discovered and Sucre quickly grabs his mirror, checking outside.

SUCRE   : We're good.

Michael slowly gets up onto his knees and squeezes through the small opening to show a maintenance area, passageway, behind the cells.
He looks around.

수감자   : (목소리) **닥쳐!**

다른 수감자들이 합세하여 소리를 질러댄다. 마이클은 미소를 지으며 콘크리트로 돌아선다. 그는 줄로 깎아낸 벽을 자신의 아프지 않은 발로 차기 시작한다. 수감자들의 떠드는 소리가 그가 내는 소음을 감싼다.
버저가 세차게 울린다.

79. 내부. 링컨의 감방. 밤
링컨은 감방 문이 열리는 소리와 결합된 그 소음을 들을 수 있다. 그의 눈은 잠에서 번쩍 뜨이고 악몽을 회상하면서 벌떡 일어난다.

80. 내부. 마이클의 감방. 밤
수크레의 노래는 A동 지역에 더 크게 울려 퍼진다. 마이클은 벽을 차 뚫어낸다. 수크레가 갑자기 멈춘다.

81. 내부. 감방 블록. 밤
교도관들이 마루 바닥으로 걸어 나온다.

벨 릭   : (소리를 지르며) **입 다물어! 이제부터 입 여는 놈은 독방 행이다!**

교도관들이 다시 급히 떠난다.

82. 내부. 마이클의 감방. 밤
마이클과 수크레는 그들이 발견될까봐 겁에 질린 표정이고, 수크레는 재빨리 거울을 집어들고 밖을 조사한다.

수크레   : **안전해.**

마이클은 천천히 무릎을 꿇고 일어나 작은 구멍을 통해 비집고 들어가 감방 뒤편에 있는 보수 지역인 통로를 본다.
그는 주위를 살핀다.

- **file**
  ~을 줄로 쓸다, 줄로 깎아내다, 자르다
  - to cut or shape something or make something smooth using a file

- **couple**
  결부시키다, 연결시키다
  - to join together two parts of something, for example two vehicles or pieces of equipment

- **maintenance**
  보수 관리, 유지, 수리, 정비, 보존
  - the act of keeping something in good condition by checking or repairing it regularly
  - the act of making a state or situation continue

- **passageway**
  복도, 낭하, 통로

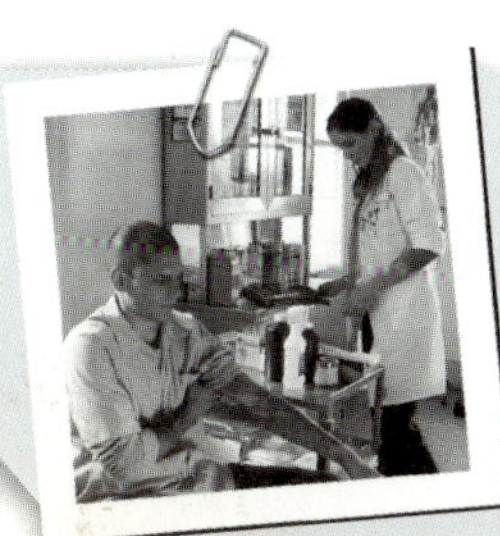

Not one more word!
더 이상 말하지 마!

▶ You must not say one more word!를 줄인 표현이다.

83. INT. AGENT HALE'S HOUSE. NIGHT
He eats dinner with his son, daughter and Allison, his pregnant wife.
Hale seems distracted.

ALLISON   : You okay?

She sits at the table.

HALE   : Work. It's fine.

He fiddles with his fork. The doorbell rings and both Hale and Allison get up to
answer it.

HALE   : I got it.

He jumps up and goes to the front door to see Kellerman standing on the porch.

HALE   : Everything all right?
KELLERMAN   : Couldn't be better.
HALE   : Do you wanna come in? We just sat down to eat.
KELLERMAN   : No. I just wanted to stop by to tell you in person.

84. EXT. HALE'S HOUSE. NIGHT
Hale steps out and shuts the door behind him.

KELLERMAN   : Problem solved.

Kellerman passes Hale some paperwork.

83. 내부. 헤일 요원의 집. 밤
그는 아들, 딸, 그리고 임신한 아내인 앨리슨과 저녁을 먹고 있다.
헤일은 마음이 산란한 것 같다.

앨리슨   : 당신 괜찮아요?

그녀는 식탁에 앉는다.

헤 일   : 일 때문이지 뭐. 괜찮아.

그는 자신의 포크를 손가락으로 무의미하게 움직인다. 현관의 벨이 울리자 헤일과 앨리슨이 둘 다 일어나 나가려고 한다.

헤 일   : 내가 나갈게.

그는 벌떡 일어나 앞문으로 가서 켈러먼이 현관이 서 있는 것을 본다.

헤 일   : 무슨 일 있어요?
켈러먼   : 더할 나위 없이 좋아.
헤 일   : 들어 오실래요? 막 식사하려던 참인데.
켈러먼   : 아니. 직접 해 주고 싶은 말이 있어서 들렀어.

84. 외부. 헤일의 집. 밤
헤일이 집 밖으로 나오며 문을 닫는다.

켈러먼   : 골칫덩이는 해결됐어.

켈러먼은 헤일에게 서류를 건넨다.

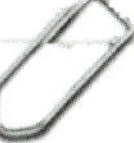

■ **distracted**
마음이 산란한, 주위가 빗나간
- unable to pay attention to somebody/something, because you are worried or thinking about something else

■ **fiddle**
(손가락으로) 가지고 놀다, 손가락을 무의미하게 움직이다
- to keep touching or moving something with your hands, especially because you are bored or nervous
- to play music on the violin

■ **in person**
자기 스스로, 실물로, 직접

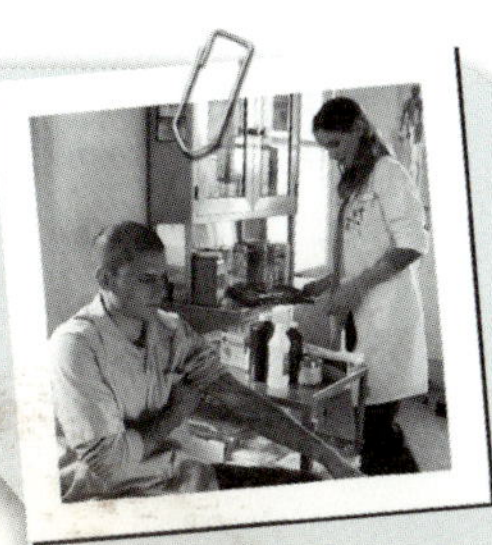

Couldn't be better.
더할 나위 없이 좋다.

▶ Everything couldn't be better.로 최상급의 뜻이며, 구어체에서 흔한 표현이다.

HALE : What's this?

KELLERMAN : That is a transfer request. Michael Scofield is getting shipped out tomorrow.

Kellerman smiles and Hale smiles dutifully back. They shake hands. Kellerman walks off.

KELLERMAN : Have a good night.

Hale's smile turns into a frown. He walks back inside.
The camera shot goes through the tunnels of the prison.

헤 일   : 이게 뭔데요?

켈러먼   : 이감 요청서야. 마이클 스코필드는 내일 다른 교
             도소로 이감된다.

켈러먼이 미소 짓자 헤일도 의무적으로 미소로 답한다. 그들은 악수를 한다.
켈러먼이 자리를 뜬다.

켈러먼   : 잘 자라고.

헤일의 미소는 찌푸림으로 변한다. 그는 집 안으로 걸어 들어간다.
카메라는 교도소의 터널을 통해 달린다.

■ **ship out**
~을 전속시키다, (배 등으로) 외국으로
보내다
- send somebody to other place

■ **dutifully**
충실하게, 예의바르게
- dutiful
  의무를 다하는, 충성된, 본분을 지
  키는
  - doing everything that you are
    expected to do
  - willing to obey and to show
    respect

치밀하게 계산된 '문신'은
제3의 주인공이다

링컨은 전기의자에서 사라지는 악몽에 시달리는 가운데 마이클 앞에는 수크레 대신 새로운 감방 동료가 된 정신 분열증 환자 헤이와이어가 나타나 새로운 장애물로 떠오른다. 그가 바로 마이클의 몸에 새겨진 문신에 대해 의심을 갖고 그 비밀을 캐기 위해 계속 마이클을 괴롭히는 것이다. 마이클은 결국 자해를 해서 헤이와이어를 내쫓는 데 성공하며 수크레와 다시 감방 동료가 되고 본격적으로 감방 벽을 뚫기 시작한다.

여기에서 드러나듯이 마이클의 문신은 치밀하게 짜여진 각본의 중추 역할을 한다. 첫 에피소드의 첫 장면에서 주인공인 마이클이 문신을 하는 장면을 설정한 이유가 여기에 있다. 물론 문신에 대한 배려는 여기서 그치지 않는다. 마이클이 폭스 리버 교도소에 수감되는 날 옷을 벗고 신체검사를 받는 장면에서도 마이클 이외의 다른 죄수가 상반신에 문신을 하고 등장한다. 수감자들에게는 흔한 광경을 통해 톱니바퀴처럼 돌아가는 파워 게임, 두뇌 게임, 유혹 게임, 탈옥 게임의 중심에 서 있는 문신… 한 치 앞도 내다 볼 수 없을 정도로 뒤통수를 치는 사건들이 일어나고 새로운 사실들이 밝혀지는 가운데에서도 사랑하는 형의 탈옥 계획의 열쇠를 쥐고 있는 문신… 이것이 이 작품을 보는 매력 가운데 한 가지 요소임에 틀림없을 것이다.

　건축 설계사이자 형이 감금되어 있는 교도소의 설계에 관여했고, 나사 하나도 어디에 있는지 알고 있는 마이클… 설계도를 훤히 알고 있을 뿐만 아니라 자신의 몸에 지니고 있다. 그게 바로 문신의 실체인 것이다. 물론 이를 바탕으로 마이클은 교도소장, 마피아, 교도관과 죄수들, 주변 인물들도 다 꿰뚫고 있고 치밀하고 완벽한 계획을 가지고 있으면서도, 우연과 운명, 각종 사고와 인간 본성 등으로 인해 계획을 매번 수정할 수밖에 없기는 하지만…

　이처럼 마이클의 반신 문신은 이 시리즈를 관통하는 토픽의 근저에 위치하는 제3의 주인공이다. 그는 탈옥이란 정교한 계획을 세우면서 그것의 세세한 부분을 정확하게 기억하기 위해서 많은 계획을 문신 속에 숨겨 둔다. 그의 탈옥 계획에서 가장 중요한 24개의 특정 디자인을 하나의 문신으로 만들어 상반신에 새겨 넣었다. 이 24개의 디자인 초안은 시즌 2에서 FBI 특수 요원인 알렉산더 마혼에 의해 마이클의 컴퓨터 하드 드라이브에서 발견된다. 문신 속에 탈옥 계획을 숨기는 아이디어는 주인공이 본 어느 피자 배달부의 문신에서 비롯된다. 문신의 스케치는 그리스어 알파벳 알파와 오메가까지로 구성되어 있다. 제작 기간 중 문신을 하나 그리는 데 약 5시간이 소요되었다. 진짜 새기는 것이 아니라 매주 그렸다고 한다. 200시간과 2만 달러의 경비가 소요되었다.

　그렇다면 마이클의 탈옥 계획을 담고 있는 문신들은 어떤 내용을 포함하고 있을까? 적어도 시즌 1에서는 마이클의 특정 문신들이 해당 에피소드와 관계를 설정하면서 자주 소개되고 있으므로 이를 추적해보도록 한다.

Allen Schweitzer 11121147

에피소드 1에서 전체적인 문신을 소개한 후
에피소드 2의 제목이기도 한 이 문신은 마
이클이 탈출하는 데 가장 기본적으로 필요한
자료이다. 그의 감방 화장실을 뜯어내고 벽
까지 가는 데에 핵심적인 볼트를 제거하기

위한 Allen Key를 나타내고 있다. 시리얼 넘버 11121147의 슈바이처 볼트
를 가지고 그는 키를 만들어 내는 데 성공한다. Schweitzer에서 i의 점은
Allen Key를 정확하게 어디까지 깎아야 하는지를 특정하게 나타내고 있다.

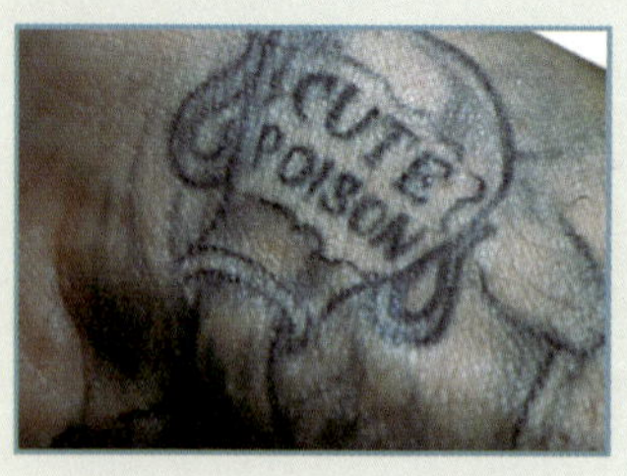

Cute Poison

에피소드 4의 제목인 '짜릿한 독극물(Cute
Poison)'이 보여주는 것처럼 문신의 내용은 중
요하다. 괴짜인 헤이와이어의 집요한 추적으
로 문신의 실체가 드러날 정도에 처한 가운데
아브루치의 도움으로 화학 약품을 구한 마이클은 짜릿한 독극물을 만들어 의무
실 지하의 파이프를 비밀스럽게 부식시키는 약품으로 사용한다. 이 파이프는
탈출의 마지막 단계로 예정되어 있다.

여기에서는 3H2SO4(aq) + Ca3(PO4)2(aq) + 6H2O(1) + 2H3PO4(aq)
+ 3CaSO4(aq) + 2H2O(1)란 화학식이 그 핵심이 된다. Cute Poison은 위
의 화학식을 가진 무수인산의 일종으로 마이클은 두 가지 방법을 이용하여
이것을 만들어 내는 데 성공한다.

English, Fitz or Percy

에피소드 5의 제목인 English, Fitz or Percy가 보여주는 것처럼 문신에서
가장 두드러졌던 내용인 이 단어들은 경찰이 교도소로 진입하기 위해 이용해

야 하는 도로의 이름들이다. 따라서 마이클은 탈출하기 전에 진입하는 경찰을 피하기 위해서 어떤 도로가 유용한지를 알아내야 한다. 경보를 울린 후 마이클은 교도소 지붕에 올라가 출동하는 경찰들이 English가와 Percy가로 도착하는 것을 본다. 빈 채로 남아 있는 도로는 Fitz뿐이다.

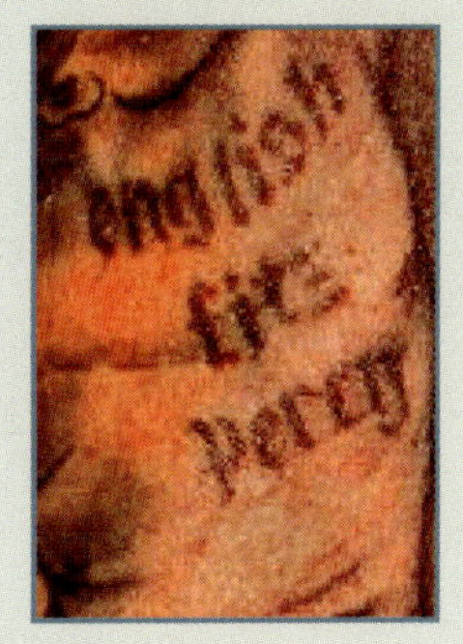

악마의 얼굴 문양

에피소드 6에서는 수감자들의 난동을 틈 타 마이클이 종이 악마의 문양을 본떠서 감방의 콘크리트 벽에 붙인다. 이 문양은 벽을 어떻게 부숴야 하는지를 보여주는 안내 그림이다. 훅의 법칙을 이용하여 가스 파이프를 건드리지 않고 벽의 주 압력 지점을 뚫을 수 있게 수학적으로 정확하게 계산하여 표시해 놓은 악마 얼굴의 특정 부분을 뚫는 것이다. 이 악마의 얼굴은 원래 십자가의 예수 형상이었는데 벽에 투사된 영상에 구멍을 뚫게 되어 있어 폭스사는 그게 종교계에 불쾌감을 줄까 염려한 나머지 악마의 얼굴로 바꾼 것이다. 미국에서도 방송심의위원회는 종교에 관한 한 진지하여, 발가락을 자르는 등 별별 폭력 장면은 다 넣어도 예수 그리스도란 말은 못 쓰게 한다나… 예수란 말도 마찬가지란다.

1 312 909 3529

이 숫자 문신은 마이클이 은행 강도죄로 체포되기 하루 전에 결혼한 Nika Volek의 전화번호이다. 마이클은 그가 원하는 것을 건네 받기 위해 전화를 한다.

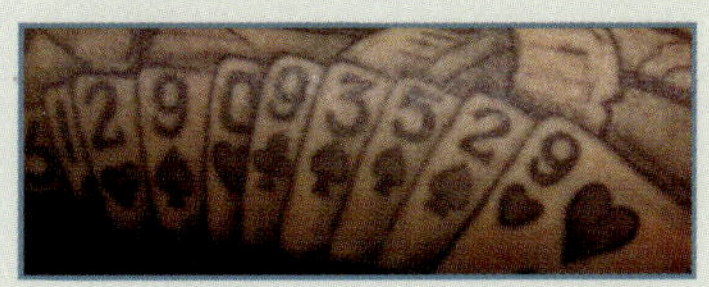

페르난도 수크레
(Fernando Sucre)

마이클 스코필드의 폭스 리버 교도소 첫 셀메이트로 인정이 많고 사람들과도 잘 지내는 라틴 아메리카 출신의 수감자다. 얼굴도 호감형이고 자신의 여자를 사랑할 줄 아는 멋진 남자로 나온다. 약간 성격이 불 같은 면이 없지 않지만 그래도 정이 가는 인물임에는 틀림없으며, 스페인어를 자주 사용하는 인물이다.

사랑하는 여인 마리크루즈에게 프러포즈하기 위해 편의점에서 반지를 훔치다가 5년형을 선고받고 수감된 그는 이제 몇 달만 있으면 풀려나는 입장이어서 처음에는 마이클의 탈옥 권유를 거부하며 다른 감방으로 도피하지만, 마리크루즈가 자기 아이를 임신한 상태로 자신의 바람둥이 사촌과 어쩔 수 없이 결혼한다는 얘기를 듣고 마이클과 함께 탈옥하기로 결심하고 오히려 그의 탈옥을 적극적으로 돕는다. 마이클이 형을 제외하고 유일하게 믿는 친구이며 감옥 내에서도 적이 없는 따뜻한 인물이다. 그가 마리크루즈와 사랑을 나누는 장면은 그야말로 순박하고 아름답다.

도둑질을 할 때도 자기가 필요한 만큼만 훔치는 착한 심성(?)의 캐릭터이며, 어떤 면에서 치밀하고 차가운 마이클보다 미소가 넉넉한 그가 더 매력 있게 비친다. 몸의 근육 또한 멋져 툭하면 옷을 벗어 던지는 역할로 등장하여 여성들의 인기를 많이 받고 있다.

그는 실제로 마이클의 반향판 같은 존재로 마이클의 인물 묘사를 하는데 결정적인 역할을 하는 인물이다. 극의 설정상 마이클이 링컨과 오랜 시간 대화할 수 없는 상황이므로 관객에게 마이클이나 링컨에 대한 정보를 드러내야 할 때면 수크레에게 바보 같은 질문을 하게 하여 사건이나 인물들에 대한 정보를 제공하는 것이다.

아마우리 놀라스코
(Amaury Nolasco)

최근 웬트워스 밀러가 미국 L.A.에 위치한 명소 힐헤이븐 로지에서 제일모직 브랜드인 빈폴의 광고 이미지 촬영을 하는 현장을 방문해 화제를 일으키기도 했던 아마우리 놀라스코(Amaury Nolasco)는 1970년 12월 24일생으로 푸에르토리코에서 태어난 배우이다. 신장이 179cm로, 의사가 되기 위해 푸에르토리코 대학에서 생물학을 공부하였으나 한 CF 감독의 눈에 띄어 발탁이 되자 뉴욕으로 이주하여 미영 드라마 예술학교에서 연기 수업을 받았다. 1999년 TV 시리즈 〈알리스〉로 데뷔했으며, 'CSI', 'ER', 'Eve', 'Mind of Mencia' 등 10여 편의 텔레비전 드라마에 출연했고, 〈분노의 질주〉(2003), 〈미스터 3000〉(2004), 〈더 벤치워머스〉(2006), 〈트랜스포머스〉(2007) 등 6편의 영화에 출연했다. 별명이 라틴 브란도(라틴의 말론 브란도)일 정도로 연기 스타일이 직관적이면서도 생생하다. 상당히 자유분방한 연기자로 정평이 나 있다. 그는 USA Today지가 발행한 '2004년에 지켜봐야 할 26명의 명사 리스트'에 Justin Timberlake, Ashton Kutcher, Josh Harnett, Jake Gyllenhaal 등의 인재들과 함께 포함되기도 했다.

프리즌 브레이크 에피소드 5에서 계속됩니다.